Behan
In The USA

Behan
In The USA

The Rise And Fall
Of The Most Famous
Irishman In New York

Dave Hannigan

Ballpoint Press

For my brother Tom and my niece Kadie

Published in 2014 by Ballpoint Press
4 Wyndham Park, Bray, Co Wicklow, Republic of Ireland.
Telephone: 00353 86 821 7631
Email: ballpointpress1@gmail.com
Web: www.ballpointpress.ie

ISBN 978-0-9926732-0-8

© Copyright Dave Hannigan, 2014

All rights reserved. No part of this publication may be reproduced,
stored in a retrieval system, or in any form or by any means,
without the prior permission in writing of the publisher, nor be
otherwise circulated in any form of binding or cover other than that
in which it is published and without a similar condition including
this condition being imposed on the subsequent publisher.

While every effort has been made to ensure the accuracy of
all information contained in this book, neither the author
nor the publisher accept liability for any errors or omissions made.

Book design and production by Elly Design

Cover photograph
Brendan Behan arrives at Pier 90, West 50th Street, Manhattan
aboard the Cunard Liner Queen Elizabeth on March 13, 1961.
PHOTO BY FRED MORGAN/NEW YORK DAILY NEWS ARCHIVE VIA GETTY IMAGES

Printed and bound by GraphyCems

Contents

Prologue

ON March 20th, 1965, the publisher Bernard Geis and the journalist Leonard Lyons were among those who gathered outside the Chelsea Hotel on West 23rd Street between Seventh and Eighth Avenues in New York. Friends of Brendan Behan, they came together for the unveiling of a plaque near the entrance to the last place he lived in the city. On the first anniversary of his death, on this simple, rectangular memorial placed upon the pillars, they had engraved the following quote from Behan, "To America, my new-found land: The man that hates you hates the human race."

It stands there still.

CHAPTER ONE

A New York State Of Mind

I hope it is clearly understood when I come to New York in September that I am allergic to shovels, and do not want to go tunneling under the East River in case it gives me the shakes – I know a more amiable way to get them. I would like to see the Rockefellers' paintings by Diego Rivera. I would also like to see the Rockefeller who said that he would like to see me in Ireland. I would like to see and pay my respects to Big Daddy Burl Ives, Lee Tracy, Studs Lonigan, Tom Lehrer, the Empire State Building, the St. Patrick's Day Parade on Fifth Avenue, Costello's Saloon on Third Avenue, Robert Frost, Marilyn Monroe, back and front, the most unforgettable character you know, the Mafia, the Mizrachi, the Daughters of the American Revolution, the Ivy League, the Niagara Falls, Nick the Greek, the Governor's pitch in Albany, William Faulkner, the Yankee Stadium, a love nest, a hot dog stand, a jam session, the Golden Gloves, and the candidates for the presidential election.

BRENDAN BEHAN, NEW YORKER MAGAZINE, SEPTEMBER 1960

DURING the first few weeks of autumn 1959, the guest list for Edward R. Murrow's Sunday afternoon talk show, "Small World", included, among others, Senator John F. Kennedy, poet Robert Frost, actress Siobhan McKenna, Israeli Prime Minister David Ben-Gurion, and Viscount Montgomery of Alamein. For Murrow's November 8th edition then, the presence of comedian Jackie Gleason, literary critic John Mason Brown (most famous for deriding comic books as the marijuana of the nursery), and emerging Irish playwright

Brendan Behan raised few eyebrows. Just a typically eclectic line-up brought together to discuss "the art of conversation".

With his play "The Hostage" scheduled to debut on Broadway in September, 1960, the programme offered Behan the perfect opportunity to introduce himself to an American television audience. CBS booked a studio in Ardmore from which he would converse with Gleason in Poughkeepsie, Mason Brown in New York and Murrow who was anchoring the show from London. Upon arrival, Behan was met by Pat Bernie, an English production assistant, a woman charged by the network with the difficult job of ensuring the most mercurial of the guests behaved himself. Some reports say he came to the studio with drink on board. Others suggest he had a bottle with him that he swigged from on set. Whatever the truth, all agree mayhem ensued.

"The art of conversation is gone," roared Behan at one point, "murdered by lunatics, most of them in the United States."

If that was hardly the type of repartee designed to endear himself to Americans tuning in for a first glimpse of the Irish playwright who had been making so many waves in London over the previous few years, there was more.

"Americans," he bellowed, "they're like a broken bicycle saddle, they'd give you a pain in your derriere."

The fact the one-liners were being delivered in a slurred Dublin accent by a man whose eyes were heavy-lidded and almost shut merely added to the theatre of the performance. Not to mention the attendant drama he brought to the mechanics of the production.

"When the programme began and the boom man swung [Behan's] microphone out of camera range, Behan rose in hot pursuit; every time it moved away from him, he shouted, to the amusement of millions of viewers, 'No, you don't, come back here', chasing the mike as though it were a canary on the loose," wrote Fred W. Friendly, producer of the show.

More than once, as one of his fellow guests spoke, Behan interjected, shouting, "Edward, Edward, where are you?" The crew moved to calm him down and to assure him Murrow was still around. The technology of the remote interview was still new back then and perhaps that bit more difficult to understand for somebody under the influence.

"How am I coming through?" asked Behan.

"You are coming through 100 per cent proof," said Gleason, obviously relishing the comedy of the moment.

"We're being killed by an Irish mob," observed the legendarily taciturn Mason Brown, clearly not enamoured with the antics coming from Dublin.

At that time, "Small World" was filmed on 35mm reels which had only 10 or 11 minutes of running time. The changing of the reels required several breaks in filming. During the first interval, Behan broke into song and then started chasing Bernie around the studio. Brown frowned at this carry-on while Gleason and Murrow couldn't help guffawing. After another reel-change, Behan was cut off. Murrow, turning back into the smooth professional instead of giggling like a naughty schoolboy at his guest's antics, told viewers the show would have to go on without him due to "circumstances beyond our control."

Another member of the backroom staff later told reporters: "There did not seem to be complete communication between the three guests, and so it was decided to continue with only two."

Gleason and Brown carried on regardless.

"It's not an act of God, it's an act," said Mason Brown in reference to Behan's sudden disappearance.

"It's an act of Guinness," said Gleason, still trying to wring comedy from the whole episode.

Back in Dublin, Behan was initially perplexed when told the shoot was over but when he later discovered what had really happened, he was furious.

"They had no right to cut me off," he said. "They never told me there was any defect in their recording apparatus. If there was any fault it wasn't mine."

With almost four weeks between recording and transmission, Friendly was so concerned about what happened he called in his boss Sig Mickelson, a legendary figure known as "the man who invented television news", to review the footage. They agreed it didn't look good but with a judicious edit it would be still possible to run it. Only when Friendly and Mickelson watched the broadcast at their homes on Sunday, November 8th did both men realise they'd made a huge mistake. Behan looked and sounded out of control and drunk. Next morning, CBS went into damage control mode, having to mollify the advertisers, especially Olin-Mathieson, a chemical company who sponsored the programme.

The fall-out went way beyond the 115 viewers who called in to complain. The Associated Press described Behan as "stoned" as he occasionally burst into "unintelligible song" yet lamented that the show was a lot duller after he'd been removed from the fray. The New York Times opted for the adjectives "spirited and incoherent" to describe his performance. The New York Daily News thought the whole thing disgraceful and accused Behan of giving "the best imitation of rambling alcoholism you ever saw." The New York World-Telegram & Sun went farthest, lambasting all involved for taking advantage of what they felt was a very sick man.

Beatrice Behan felt her husband had been the victim of censorship while Behan himself remained irate at how he he'd been edited out, reduced to a bit-part player in the discussion.

"I don't suppose Mason Brown liked me calling him a liar, any more than the Americans would like to hear that the art of conversation went out when the atom bomb came in, because it has been murdered by lunatics, mostly from the United States," said Behan, completely oblivious to the part he might have played in his own downfall.

It didn't matter too much that all the protagonists had different opinions and versions of what happened because the upshot of the whole brouhaha was very obvious; America had just been exposed for the first time to a glimpse of Brendan Behan in all his glory. They would not have to wait too much longer to gain a more extended and revealing look at the man behind the growing legend.

On August 31st, 1960, Colin Frost from the Associated Press interviewed Brendan Behan as he packed his bags for his first trip to America, ahead of the New York opening of "The Hostage" at the Cort Theatre on September 20th. After months of well-publicised sobriety, the reporter still thought it relevant enough to lead the story with the image of Behan stuffing bottles of soda water into his suitcase, in between the shirts and socks.

"It's great stuff, sometimes I even think I like it," said Behan, spawning the inevitable newspaper headline, "Water? It's Great Says Behan!" This was above an article in which he held forth on the impact of this new abstemious regime on his health. "Since I took to the water instead of the liquor, I've lost 28lbs and 11 teeth. The loss of weight is self-explanatory. The teeth were always aching but when I was on the jag I didn't notice it. When I went dry, they had to come out."

Two days later, Behan boarded a plane for Idlewild Airport in New York, accompanied by Beatrice and the cast of the play, including his sister-in-law Celia Salkeld, an actress who was to play Teresa in the production. A notoriously nervous flyer (her later transatlantic trips would be made by ship), Beatrice wasn't at all thrilled at the prospect of a lengthy sojourn in New York. She didn't share her husband's childish excitement at the thought of seeing a city he'd read about and seen so much of in movies over the years. And she had told him so when the trip was first mooted.

"He was eager to embrace people of all kinds, and New York had people of more kinds than any place else in the world," wrote Beatrice. "When he asked me what I thought, I told him New York was like a giant fun fair. Success was obviously more resounding here, yet I imagined that failure could be catastrophic."

From the moment he walked on board the plane, Behan's fellow passengers could have been forgiven for believing he had fallen spectacularly off the wagon and made a liar of the fresh newspaper reports of his new sober persona. Befitting a man-child setting off on a great adventure to a promised land, he was in gregarious and uproarious form, despite the fact not a drop of alcohol had passed his lips. Indeed, he sipped soda water laced with lime juice throughout and ate everything put in front of him, including meals given to Beatrice who couldn't face food en route due to her nervousness.

"Whenever I travel anywhere on a plane, it always seems to be full of fucking nuns," Behan shouted, after spotting a group of nuns taking their seats. "And they take the vow of poverty."

That wasn't to be his only run in with people of the faith either.

"Why don't you have one of your plays running at the Dublin festival, Mr. Behan?" asked a priest later in the flight.

"Same reason as you're not married, father," said Behan. "Nobody asked me!"

The boisterousness might have been born of fear of flying

or just his natural inclination to perform for a crowd, there being no more captive audience for a showman than the passengers on a plane traversing the Atlantic Ocean.

"The journey was terrifying," wrote Victor Spinetti, an English actor who was heading to New York to reprise his London role in the production as an IRA officer. "First the plane skimmed the waves, then it rocked and dived. Headwinds blew us back, and direct flight or no direct flight, we had to land and refuel. Brendan said, 'We'd better get up a concert party, all do turns to cheer ourselves up.'"

So that is what they did. Spinetti offered an impression of Alec Guinness playing Lawrence of Arabia in Terence Rattigan's play "Ross", and Behan threw himself into the impromptu festivities too. He delivered a beautiful rendition of "Paper Pins" and then a rousing version of "The Auld Triangle", the prison anthem from his play "The Quare Fellow". The irony of the second song was obvious. Here was somebody who knew the inside of jails and cells all too well, now flying across the ocean for the Broadway premiere of his second major play in the media capital of the world.

It was a measure of his standing and his sobriety that the captain invited him up to the flight deck as the plane began its descent into New York, a city eagerly anticipating his arrival. That much was evident by the scrum of journalists who greeted him when he eventually touched down at Idlewild. Clutching a box from Shannon Airport, he paused on the steps of the Aer Lingus Irish International Airlines Lockheed Constellation so the cameramen could capture his arrival.

"We were hot by the time Brendan and the company arrived, long overdue, but the crowd of reporters still growing," wrote Joan Littlewood, the director of "The Hostage" who'd flown in from London a week earlier. "Even before the landing steps were in place, he was at the door smiling and waving. The rush was on. He was lost in a forest of cameras and microphones. I caught a glimpse of him, trotting across the tarmac, an enormous rosette in his buttonhole. The company looked a bit shaky. They'd been 14 hours in the air. Two nuns and a priest brought up the rear."

The flight might have taken 14 wearying hours to complete but Behan wasn't too tired to perform for the flash bulbs and the reporters. Indeed, it seemed like he was invigorated by them. Wearing a dark brown, two-tone suit, he had an "Up Down" rosette in his right lapel. Fans of the Down Gaelic footballers had worn them during their All-Ireland semi-final victory over Offaly at Croke Park a couple of weeks earlier and Behan loved the contradictoriness of the slogan. If he thought the badge might come in handy as a conversation piece, he, of course, didn't need one. From the moment the New York press came into earshot, he was firing off one-liners on every topic imaginable.

"I'm not a politician because I have only one face," he said when they asked about his views on the presidential election before then, of course, offering an opinion. "I'm for Kennedy because he's of the Roosevelt Party and Roosevelt was a great man."

Then there was a question about the Catholic Church regarding some of his work as blasphemous.

"I'll invite Cardinal Spellman and Billy Graham and the rabbi if he wants to come to my play. In health, I'm not very religious. When I'm sick, I'm very religious! On the airplane, a nun sat next to me. There were moments when I felt like snatching the rosary beads out of her hands and doing a little praying myself."

In between the scattershot repartee, he offered humility too.

"Appearing on Broadway is like an athlete running the four minute mile! It is something whether the play is a success or not. It's exciting and thrilling. I'm not a good enough actor to be blasé about it. I've been asked to be civil to the critics, those butchers of Broadway. I intend to step out of their road and see what happens. It [Broadway] is a place of legend, like Killarney or Montmarte, in different ways. One confidently expects to see Damon Runyon's Harry the Horse and the girls banging the drums and blowing the trumpets for the dolls."

Given that America's only prolonged encounter with him to date had been his drunken appearance on "Small World", the questioning inevitably turned to drink.

"I will drink tea, coffee and soda water while I'm in America," said Behan. From somewhere, a pitcher of milk and a glass was produced. Behan scrunched his face up as if disgusted by the very idea before taking a sip and quipping: "I may need a stomach pump." Then he held the glass up for the clicking cameras and assured reporters the five bottles of whiskey he had in his case were not for him but were gifts for American friends. Indeed, he mentioned that he was unsure about going on a proposed lecture tour across the country unless he could "do it without having to get drunk afterwards." He even offered an honest appraisal of the extent of his problem.

"The trouble with me is that I can't drink just a small quantity a day, say a pint of whiskey and 12 bottles of stout. I can't stop drinking and I become a bore and a nuisance and begin to say things, some of them of an obscene nature."

Now cognisant of his failings, he assured the press there would be no more of him interrupting the live performances of the play, something the productions of his work in London had become infamous for.

"No because somebody would say to me, 'Listen, Mac, I paid $5 to see this show, not to see you drunk.' An English audience is tough, it contains people who have been to public schools, Brixton Prison and Wormwood Scrubs, and sometimes to all three. But American audiences are gentle and you've got to treat them gently."

The press lapped up this newly self-aware and contrite version of Behan, remarking on the healthy colour of his skin, his pugnacious jaw and, of course, his recently-discovered love of temperance.

"Brendan blows in, still dry!" announced one headline. "Behan vows to shun old John Barleycorn!" went another.

At one point that day at Idlewild, Jinx Falkenburg, a former cover girl and tennis star turned influential broadcaster, stuck a microphone under his chin.

"And what else do you want to do in New York, Mister Behan?" she asked.

"Go down to the YMHA and take a swim in the pool."

"Why the YMHA, the Young Men Hebrew's Association? I mean, you aren't Jewish, are you Brendan?"

"No," he replied. "But I'll be famous down there. Not because I'm a playwright but because I'll have the only foreskin in the pool."

The journalists guffawed, partly at the gag, partly at how easy this Irish guy was making their job. He was giving them zinger after zinger.

"One of the policemen just said to me that being a celebrity I was probably well accustomed to a police escort. 'Yes,' says I, 'though usually with handcuffs.'"

Too often, international sensations arrived in New York and, cowed by the bright lights of the big city, they underwhelmed the local media, a bunch who'd seen and heard it all before. Behan blew in like a breath of fresh air, practically doing their job for them.

"Do you think you'd like to address the Women's Christian Temperance Union?" somebody asked from behind the phalanx of microphones.

"Well I'd tell them to look a bit more cheerful, the H Bomb isn't going to be dropped all that quick," he replied to raucous laughter.

The reviews of his debut performance were predictably effusive.

"Brendan Behan, the uninhibited, fun-loving Irish playwright with the awesome reputation for quaffing the 'sauce,' arrived in New York yesterday as sober as the proverbial judge and as amiable as a vote-getting politician," wrote Louis Calta in the New York Times. "The author said he planned to remain in New York until Christmas. But if his play failed to receive the support of the public and critics, he planned to join the Fire Department!"

Leonard Field, one of the producers bringing "The Hostage" to America, turned to Beatrice at the airport said, "They've fallen in love with Brendan."

Field knew that, aside from the advance praise from London, the most effective promotional tool of all had just arrived in town. Over the course of the next two weeks, Behan did more than 50 interviews. That he was reworking some old lines and offering a few that would become staples of his act in America over the next three years mattered not a jot to the New York media. Everybody was too taken with the novelty of the new show in town, and the charm offensive was necessary too because there had been plenty of negative stories doing the rounds about his legendary capacity to cause trouble.

Yet, here he was, larger than life and twice as loud. A question about his membership of the Irish Republican Army was met with a double-barrelled reply. First there was the standard response he'd been offering for years.

"They sentenced me to death in me absence. 'Right,' I said, 'you can shoot me in my absence.'"

They jotted down the gags between laughs and buoyed by the response, Behan offered them the second part of his answer to the question by bursting into a verse from "The Laughing Boy", his lament for Michael Collins which he'd written at the age of 13!

Oh had he died by Pearse's side or in the GPO
Killed by an English bullet from the rifle of the foe
Or forcibly fed where Ashe lay dead
In the dungeons of Mountjoy
I'd have cried with pride
At the way you died
My own dear laughing boy

"The questioning went on for four hours," wrote Littlewood in what was something of an exaggeration. "Every time Gerry (Raffles – her partner) moved in to put a stop to it the newshounds bayed for more and by now, BB wanted to give it to them. He ran his fingers through his tousled hair, in his element, entertaining that tough audience. We had to drag him away."

During the build-up to Behan's arrival it had fallen to Field to persuade Andrew Anspach, manager of the Algonquin Hotel on 44th Street between Fifth and Sixth Avenue, to allow the playwright to stay at an establishment famed for its literary associations since Dorothy Parker and the Round Table convened there back in the 1920s. If hosting the finest writers of several generations had made the hotel synonymous with creative genius through the ensuing decades, Anspach had heard one too many stories of Behan's drunken escapades.

"The Algonquin has dignity, Leonard," he told Field. "It may be Bohemian, but it's a rather proper hotel and no place for rowdyism. It's a hotel where artists aren't just celebrated, but esteemed. He could be an embarrassment. I think we had better not chance it. Why not book him in somewhere else?

Perhaps the Chelsea? It doesn't have a residents' lounge, and it's a very good hotel, and – well – you know, more Bohemian."

"I promise you Andrew, he won't cause you any trouble," said Field, citing Behan's sobriety as evidence his days as a hell-raiser were behind him.

It certainly seemed that way when he checked into the hotel. Sober and witty and seemingly determined to live up to his advance billing, he came, trailing reporters behind him. Some had followed him in from the airport. More were waiting in the lobby. That so many journalists were deputised to cover Behan's arrival is indicative of how much his reputation preceded him. Among the throng was Leonard Lyons. The city's pre-eminent gossip column of the time, his "Lyons Den" ran six days a week in the New York Post, and in dozens of other papers nationwide. Very quickly, Behan would become a fixture in it, as the pair formed an unlikely and genuine friendship.

"I hope his kidneys hold out," Field whispered to Lyons in the lobby of the Algonquin as he entertained the reporters, a throwaway remark that betrayed how genuinely worried he was that Behan's sobriety couldn't possibly hold in New York of all places. Meanwhile, a few feet away, the man himself continued to deliver easy copy.

"I would have loved to have lived in America during the 1870s," said Behan. "I would have been a carpetbagger or a scallywag, whichever was the most obnoxious."

He knew his history and his contemporary trends too.

"What about the Beatniks? Brendan?"

"Beatniks – the thing that I have against them is that they are always looking for a job – my job!"

He wasn't as well-up on the contemporary American theatre. When asked what plays he might take in during his stay, he confessed to having no idea what else was playing. Somebody mentioned Gore Vidal's "The Best Man". "Is he an Indian?" asked Behan before then mentioning writers he did know.

"If there was anything playing by Tennessee Williams or if there was anything by Eugene O'Neill I might sneak in to get a few tips. The sort of thing I would like to see is W.C. Fields, Jimmy Durante and Will Mahoney but I guess they aren't playing now."

Obviously thrilled at how well his material was going down with the new audience, he praised the reporters for their attitude.

"Newspaper men here are not as aggressive as in London. There, they are always catching an edition. They give me the impression of always being busy."

At a certain point in that conversation, he turned to speak Irish to Beatrice.

"Is that Gaelic?" asked a reporter.

"Yes," said Behan. "We use it if we think you don't understand it!"

Perhaps predictably, the first night in New York ended in the wee small hours of the following morning in Jimmy Glennon's Bar on Third Avenue. There, still sober while all around him, cast and crew, were drinking deep of their new surroundings, Behan held forth in a venue where a sign reading, "It's better to be rich and healthy than poor and sick" hung over the bar. Beside it was a photograph of Queen Elizabeth II in familiar royal regalia except for the fact she had a black eye.

He had found a home away from home.

CHAPTER TWO

The Most Citified City In The World

New York suited Brendan's generous temperament. His talkativeness was his way of entertaining as many people as possible. His flamboyance covered his shyness. He wanted people to like and admire him...Brendan loved traipsing around New York, dropping into bars and talking to his fellow drinkers. As a writer, he was entitled to call his pleasure business. The pubs he frequented were his clubs and research centres.

CAROLINE BURKE SWANN, CO-PRODUCER OF THE HOSTAGE

FROM the moment the plane hit the tarmac at Idlewild with the presence of a media scrum confirming the size of his burgeoning celebrity, Brendan Behan fell in love with New York. It would become the one place in his life about which he only ever wrote positively and waxed lyrically. Waiting for the lift at the Algonquin Hotel one morning that first week, a fellow guest, an older woman from the Midwest, engaged him in conversation and told him that in her opinion, "New York is hell!" Behan's reply was polite yet offered a window into the affection he already evinced for his new abode.

"I've never felt so much at home anywhere as I do in New York," he said, childishly incredulous that anybody could have anything negative to say about the place.

"That could very well be," she said, a dry response that suggests she might have known exactly why the two were made for each other.

Others were coming to that realisation as well. Witness his

arrival at the offices of Bernard Geis and Associates on 72nd Street one afternoon. A former magazine editor who'd started his own publishing company with high-profile backing from friends like Groucho Marx, Alfred Bloomingdale and others, Geis had read the books, heard about the growing legend, and paid Behan a $12,000 advance for a sequel to "Borstal Boy". Even somebody immersed in the social whirl of New York as long as Geis had been got more than he bargained for when his new author decided to drop by.

"Stop work everybody," shouted Behan as he emerged from the elevator. The staff duly downed tools, partly out of respect, partly out of bemusement at the tousle-haired maniac whose voice was suddenly booming around the room. Before they could resume their tasks, he broke into song. There followed more singing, a little bit of poetry, and eventually, he even cajoled some of the women up on their feet to dance with him. If Geis had been attracted by the size of Behan's literary talent, even he was overwhelmed by the force of nature suddenly before him.

"If you're like this sober, what are you like drunk?" he asked.

"Oh, I'm the same as now, except I pass out," said Behan.

The pair became fast friends as Geis enjoyed the outsized character. One morning they were walking down a street near his office when Behan stopped to give money to a blind African-American with a seeing-eye dog.

"Very generous of you," said Geis.

"Oh it's not that," replied Behan. "I'm afraid of his big dog!"

More than most of those with commercial interests in Behan's career, Geis would prove to almost always have the Dubliner's best interests at heart. In that cameo back in the office though, as so often in the early days of that first visit to Manhattan, it seemed like Behan was drunk on the city, actually intoxicated by the sheer excitement and the irresistible glamour and the non-stop action of it all.

"I'm not afraid to admit that New York is the greatest city on the face of God's earth," he wrote later of the awe he felt for the surroundings. "You only have to look at it from the air, from the river, from Father Duffy's statue. New York is easily recognisable as the greatest city in the world, view it any way and every way – back, belly and sides....A city is a place where Man lives, walks about, talks and eats and drinks in the bright light of the day or electricity for 24 hours a day. In New York at three in the morning, you can walk about and see crowds, read the papers and have a drink – orange juice, coffee, whiskey or anything. It is the greatest show on earth, for everyone. Its fabulous beauty at night, even forty years ago, was the wonder of the world."

For a man who came trailing a reputation for combative, drunken and downright loutish behaviour that had been well-chronicled in the American press, he seemed remarkably relaxed. On his first full day in the country, when he and Beatrice came down for dinner at the Round Table restaurant in the Algonquin Hotel. Raoul, the maître d' noticed Behan was without a collar or a tie, contravening the dining room regulations. Raoul asked him to go back upstairs and return fully-dressed.

"Adjust either the weather or the clothing requirements," Behan muttered under his breath, having earlier pleaded that a man couldn't possibly wear a tie on a sweltering hot September evening in New York. But, he left and returned with a tie in place, and when it was pointed out to him the room was air-conditioned, he even admitted, "They were right then, the weather's adjusted."

If this was exactly the type of formal request that might, on a different day, have set him off, Behan was in too good form to be riled by anything at this point in his sojourn.

"I don't know myself anymore," said Behan to Leonard

Lyons, as he sipped mineral water and tucked into two large steaks.

Not only did he appear at ease, he was determined to see every inch of the place at every hour of the day and night, wringing every last drop from the experience. One minute, he was telling the New York Daily News about his experience getting fitted with a new suit for the opening night of the play, insisting that he'd warned the tailor no British fabric could be used in the making of it. In reporting this, nobody bothered to point out "The Hostage" was being put on by an East London-based theatre company with an almost entirely British cast. The small print didn't matter because the big picture was too colourful a sight to behold.

The next minute, he was putting on overalls, revisiting his previous profession and giving the office of Leonard Field, one of the producers who'd brought the play to Broadway, a coat of cream-coloured paint.

"If the play is a hit, said Field, "I'm bound to get a second coat. Even if it flops, I'll get it since Brendan will need the work. But a hit play will mean a free paint job."

The portrait is of a man who'd plugged himself into the city's grid and been energized like never before. On September 10th, Behan turned up at Jaeger House, a bar and dance hall on 85th Street and Lexington Avenue. A handsome red-brick building that once housed one of the city's most storied German restaurants and served as a meeting place for Nazi sympathisers in the 1930s, it had more recently been commandeered by the Irish. Under the ownership of Harry McGuirk whose diverse business interests in the Irish-American community included journalism, running a travel agency and DJing, it had become the go-to night-time destination for Irish men and women from all over the five boroughs.

When Behan walked in the door, Jaeger House was packed

to overflowing, the usual Saturday night crowd. And, of course, he was in his element.

"New York is the most citified city in the world!" he told reporters who'd been sent along by their editors to chronicle what Behan might do next. The answer to that question was simple; he was bent on entertaining everybody who crossed his path.

"I've been telling everyone you're my third cousin," said a young Irish woman who immediately approached him. "And they believe me."

"My God," replied Behan, "why would a pretty girl like you want me for a cousin?"

His face glistening with beads of sweat dripping down his face from the heat of too many bodies in too small a room, he cradled a glass of soda water in his hand and humoured every single drink-fuelled emigrant, or son or daughter of emigrants, who wanted to shake his hand and pat his back. Finally, he was beseeched to move to where everybody could catch a glimpse of the celebrity in their midst.

Wearing an unbuttoned sports shirt, no collar or tie, and with sweat furiously dampening it in patches, he ambled onto the stage. His pants sagging for the want of a belt around his newly slimmed waist, he eschewed the offer of a microphone, apologised for interrupting the dancing, and delivered a cupla focal as Gaeilge. Then, much to the delight of the crowd, he started into song.

'Twas down by the glenside, I met an old woman
A-plucking young nettles, she ne'er saw me coming
I listened a while to the song she was humming
Glory O, Glory O, to the bold Fenian men...

Written by his mother's brother Peader Kearney, "Down by the Glenside" went down so well that he took another from his uncle's canon, delivering a rip-roaring rendition of the nationalist anthem "Whack Fol the Diddle". During both songs, he shouted "Up the Republic!" between verses and each time, the crowd, growing ever more frenzied, shouted "Up the Republic!" right back at him. He finished his impromptu concert with "Molly Malone", by which time his shirt was almost soaked through.

"Mr. Behan is a victim of his own ebullience," wrote Arthur Gelb in a perceptive piece that appeared on the front page of the "New York Times" on September 18th. "It is his pleasure and his passion to hold court – anytime, anywhere, and for anyone. This has had a snowballing effect that has prevented him from getting much sleep. Saloonkeepers, head waiters, freshly-arrived young members of Ireland's revolutionary party, chance passersby, all have equal claim on Mr. Behan's time. For most of them he plays the clown. But Mr. Behan has another side."

That side was on show when Gelb sat down to interview Behan at the Algonquin Hotel's restaurant. Sipping ice water and puffing on a cigar, Behan was on his best behaviour for this encounter, obviously trying to make sure that the man from the Times glimpsed the full range of his linguistic talents. He had an impromptu conversation in French with the waiter working the table and then spoke Irish to Beatrice, little cameos ensuring Gelb could see there was more to this guy than the admittedly entertaining tabloid caricature.

An experienced reporter who would co-author a heavyweight biography of the playwright Eugene O'Neill, Gelb was smart enough to realise Behan (whom he accurately described as "a bawdy, iconoclastic, ballad-singing, jig-dancing, stocky, rumpled, wild-haired 37 year old") often struggled during the interview to stop himself offering the pithy response instead of the thoughtful answer. The piece that appeared ended up showcasing both sides of his character. For example, he went long on religion....

"I suppose I am inclined to believe in all that the Catholic church teaches. I am accused of being blasphemous. But blasphemy is the comic verse of belief. My sins aren't any more interesting than anyone else's. If a man is horrified by another man's sins, it is because he is uneducated, inexperienced or a hypocrite. Certain things must be restrained in the world for our convenience – but for our convenience only. Why can't we let it go at that? The nearest thing to a horrifying act in a reasonable society is a crime against a child. One thing I respect about Catholic teaching is that one mortal sin is as bad as another."

...and on life after death.

"At the end of the play, the hostage is killed – but he comes alive again. Why? Send the audience home happy. Death is vulgarised when looked upon as an end. It may be the end of this world as far as the bloke is concerned, but life goes on. I don't know what life is – whether there is a life force. I'm a very confused man. But I'm all for resurrection. There should be resurrection every week for the dead."

He went shorter but sharper on patriotism...

"Why do I ridicule my country? The first duty of a writer is to let his country down. He knows his own people the best. He has a special responsibility to let them down."

...and politicians.

"Politicians who call upon the people for sacrifice and duty to their country are dangerous. They are entitled to six ounces of lead between the eyes – not in the brain because they have no brains."

Gelb perhaps summed up Behan's immediate impact best when he described him as "already as much of a public pet here as he is in Europe." Whatever the truth of that assessment, the simple fact the editors of the New York Times deemed him front-page news after more than two hectic weeks during which he'd been a fixture in it and rival newspapers says a lot about where he now ranked in the city's cultural hierarchy. It was the kind of product placement theatre impresarios can usually only dream about two days before "The Hostage" was due to open at the Cort Theatre.

It was also an affirmation of the place he'd reached in his life. For a playwright with ambition, New York was the promised land, Broadway the pinnacle of any career. Just six years had passed since "The Quare Fellow", Behan's first play, had been produced by the small, avant-garde Pike Theatre in Dublin, at a venue that held just 50 seats. Now, here he was preparing to open "The Hostage" on the Great White Way, while being regarded as a major talent, a new, fresh and vital voice in world theatre. Just 37 years old, his journey to this point, to this city, to this level, had already been quite an extraordinary climb.

Born on February 9, 1923 in Holles Street Hospital, his first home was in Russell Street off the North Circular Road, one of Dublin's great Georgian terraces that had been allowed to lapse into decay and which, by then, were regarded as tenements. His mother Kathleen had two children from her first marriage to Jack Furlong who had died in the influenza epidemic of 1918. She married Stephen Behan in 1922 and Brendan was their first child, his arrival coming at a tough time. In a country wracked by civil war, his father had been arrested and imprisoned for anti-Treaty activities. The first he saw of his son was when Kathleen stood outside the jail and held the new baby aloft so Stephen could glimpse him through the bars on the window.

If the economic reality of his upbringing was tough, Behan grew up in a house where literature and the arts were encouraged. Of an evening Brendan and his brothers, Seamus,

Brian and Dominic (the latter pair would go on to gain fame as writers themselves) would sit around their father and hear him read to them from his favourite books. At his knee, they gained exposure at such an impressionable age to an impressive array of authors that included Charles Dickens, William Thackeray, George Bernard Shaw, Emile Zola and Giovanni Boccacio.

"His unusual parents, forced by unusual circumstances into tenement living, came from family backgrounds rather different to the majority of their neighbours," wrote Michael O'Sullivan in his excellent biography of Behan. "From his father he got his love of literature. From his mother, he got his love of song and his passionate hatred of England, a hatred that would become somewhat tempered with time and would rarely if ever extend to the ordinary English people he met."

His mother and father weren't the only major influences on him during those formative years. The building where they lived and several other slums in the area were owned by Granny English, his grandmother. From an early age, Brendan was her darling but his favourite status cut both ways. She introduced him to drink very young, using him to courier jugs of porter to her discretely from Gill's pub up the street, and, to the consternation of many in the vicinity, allowing him to get roaring drunk in her company.

"Brendan acquired his taste for spirits from his Granny as well," wrote Ulick O'Connor. "When he was eight, she fed him whiskey: 'It'll cure the worms,' she told his mother when Kathleen complained that Brendan was coming home woozy. He knew what it was to be inebriated well before his teens."

Aside from this colourful environment that gave him fecund material for his writing, it was an upbringing the like of which infused him then with his two great passions, words and drink. The pity was, of course, that the one would eventually drown the other.

His grandmother died a few months before his 13th birthday and he took it badly, the trauma soon exacerbated by the news that Russell Street had been condemned. As part of a government slum clearance initiative, the Behans were relocated to 70 Kildare Road, Crumlin, a suburb of Dublin that to them and many others in the scheme seemed as remote as the wild west. Around the same time, he left the Christian Brothers' school (where he'd displayed great promise as a writer and an upstart) and began to attend the apprentice college at Bolton Street in order to become a house painter. As roads to Broadway go, this was more circuitous than most.

Elsewhere in those teen years, there was dabbling in poetry (most of a Republican nature), an abortive attempt to join a band of Irish Republicans embarking to fight against fascism in the Spanish Civil War, and, eventually, membership of the Irish Republican Army. It was on IRA duty in Liverpool in 1939 that he was arrested and sentenced to three years at Hollesley Bay Borstal (young offenders) Institution. There was another lengthier prison sentence for firing a gun at a policeman in Dublin in 1942. For an aspiring young writer, these experiences offered a rich seam of experience that he would later mine to great effect.

Upon release from the Curragh Interment Camp in 1946, Behan worked on ships, as a housepainter and even a smuggler. There were further spells in various jails and a stint living in Paris. Along the way, he also started to dabble in journalism with The Irish Times and the Irish Press, and other forms of writing too. Yet, it wasn't until 1950 that he had tried to make it his full-time job. Even then, there were several times in the ensuing years when he had to pick up a brush and ladder to try to earn a few bob to bolster his income. Joking with Leonard Field aside, those days were well and truly over.

Now, just a decade on from resolving to try earn a living from the typewriter, he was the toast of Broadway. The New York newspapers were hanging on his every word, publishers were throwing money at him (one visitor to his hotel room recalled that the floor was papered with unopened letters), and stars were inviting him into the inner sanctum. An enviable position yet one with obvious perils.

"The pressures imposed on the unknown and the inexperienced in America are considerable," wrote Rae Jeffs, Behan's editor at Hutchison. "But for a world-famous playwright, there are no scales large enough to weigh them."

After it was first announced that "The Hostage" was transferring to New York. Behan was in a pub in Ballsbridge drinking with Desmond Mackey. When he informed his friend of his great news, Mackey didn't react as he'd hoped because instantly all he could imagine was an alcoholic on the loose in America.

"Brendan, you're fucked," he said.

"Why do you say that?" asked Behan.

"You know that don't you?"

Behan didn't have to ask any more questions. He understood what Mackey meant.

"He had been a long time in the nick, either up at the Curragh concentration camp for the IRA men, then in jail in England, then to Borstal and then he's famous," said Mackey. "You're suddenly brought up and thrown late into that in the middle of Broadway. How do you live with that?"

Mackey's gloomy prediction would be proved right eventually but for a time, Behan adapted rather quickly to the challenge of the new surroundings. In those early days, his determination not to drink was impressive, more especially because it was regularly tested.

"I remember once he wasn't drinking," said Terence Moran, then a student at New York University, who happened upon

Behan at McSorley's in the East Village "He was in at the bar and his wife was standing outside [women were not admitted until the 1970s]. A friend of mine went over and said, 'Mr Behan, I don't want to disturb you, but I just want to say how much I admire your work. I think you're a genius and I just want to buy you an ale.' So Brendan took the ale and poured it on the floor without saying anything. I think he wanted to make a dramatic gesture for his wife, who was at the door."

Sober, he was relishing the opportunity to meet some of his contemporaries, one or two of whom were also idols. One afternoon, he met Burgess Meredith in the lobby of the Algonguin. Probably best-known as an actor, Meredith was then directing a revue on Broadway called "The Thurber Carnival" that would go on to win a Tony award. Meredith was on his way up to visit James Thurber, who kept an apartment at the hotel, and Behan told him he'd love to meet the writer.

"We went up to Jim's suite and passed a night and day of torrential talk, with only brief moments of separation," wrote Meredith. "As I say, there was no drinking on Behan's part, and because he was sober, Thurber, Helen (his wife), and I were temperate too. Thurber was fascinated by Behan and Behan by Thurber. Behan had a headful of entrancing theories about Thurber's famous characters. He would imitate them, improvise their dialogue, all in a rich and very loud brogue."

The quartet were having so much fun that others guests complained to the management about the noise coming from Thurber's room. Eventually, there came a rap on the door.

"If you gentlemen were intoxicated, I would feel justified in shutting you up, but under these circumstances it is difficult, very difficult indeed," said the manager when he discovered the racket was the result of laughter rather than liquor. "Keep talking but for God's sake be quiet."

After that hectic opening encounter, Thurber later

introduced Behan to Thornton Wilder, the Pulitzer-prize winning playwright and novelist.

"Oh, sure I know Brendan Behan, I recognise him," said Wilder as they shook hands.

"Let us all sit down and have a drink, Thornton," said Thurber. "Brendan is like ourselves, he's an old pro."

These were genuine literary giants delighted to make his acquaintance. Indeed, he and Wilder would have dinner together at Brasserie again a few weeks later. A Joycean scholar, Wilder delighted in Behan telling him that his granduncle was the coachman in Ulysses. The American also liked him enough to advise that he should stay in America and never return to Dublin because the best Irish writers were always in exile. A piece of counsel Behan would use again and again when trying to persuade his wife they should move to New York permanently.

CHAPTER THREE

The Play's The Thing

Brendan, that bastard; I kicked the coffin. He didn't need a theatre. He was a walking theatre. He came from a famous republican family. The Abbey wouldn't touch him; the middle-class of Dublin called him a gutter-snipe. But I've always been a republican – not in the American sense. He sent me a playscript, covered in beer-stains that seemed to come from the first typewriter ever invented. I read it and said 'come over and let's do something about it.' He couldn't do anything himself; the word edit was not in his vocabulary.

JOAN LITTLEWOOD, 26 MARCH, 1994

IN 1953, Joan Littlewood and Gerry Raffles finally found a permanent home for Theatre Workshop, their travelling troupe which had, under one guise or another, been permanently on the road since the end of World War II. The Theatre Royal on Angel Lane in Stratford-atte-Bowe, East London had seen better days, a fact reflected in the cheap rent of just £20 per week, but, over the course of the next two decades, Littlewood and Raffles turned this unlikely venue into one of the most influential spaces in British theatre. They managed this feat with little or no money, just talent, hard work and the occasional slice of good fortune.

In the beginning, the entire company slept on the premises even though, in Littlewood's own words, the place reeked of "perfumed disinfectant and cat piss." The actors worked part-time jobs around the East End to supplement their incomes, local businesses were relentlessly tapped up for patronage, and everybody in the cast chipped in with the cleaning and the carpentry. It was the only way to refurbish and revitalise a building that was by then already almost 70 years old. Still, it was a home and it was a stage. And that was really all Littlewood needed to work her own brand of theatrical magic.

Born to a single mother in South London in 1914, Littlewood was remarkable character who emerged from those unpromising beginnings to win a scholarship to RADA where she once ended up rehearsing George Bernard Shaw's "Heartbreak House" in front of the playwright himself. Unhappy with the plum accents and snobbish attitudes prevailing in the epicentre of English dramatic scholarship back then, Littlewood decided to emigrate to America, setting off on foot to walk to Liverpool to catch a ship. After more than a hundred miles on the road, she ended up being diverted and eventually wound up in Manchester. She would reach New York and Broadway one day but only after several more hugely entertaining detours along the way.

In Manchester, she carved out a career as a producer in the BBC, married and later divorced the folk singer Ewan McColl, and began dabbling in agit-prop theatre. Her leftist political views brought her to the attention of MI5 which dubbed her "a keen communist" and after years on the highways and byways of the regional circuit, she used her first permanent base in East London to wage theatrical war on elitism and snobbery and, where possible, to promote socialism. She made a habit of thumbing her nose up at West End productions and attacking the stilted sensibility of so much post-war English theatre.

This rather tumultuous life story, the colourful background and the epic journey to centre stage had then, in so many ways, prepared this five foot two bundle of energy for the arrival in her life of one Brendan Behan, somebody whose own biography was equally action-packed and unorthodox. Few were better equipped to harness his wayward talent and unleash his irreverence upon the staid London theatre than a woman who'd spent her whole career trying to subvert that world from inside and out.

"While we were playing 'Edward II' a tattered bundle appeared on my desk," wrote Littlewood of the day in 1956 when she first read the work of Behan. "It was from Ireland and addressed to Ewan McColl who had forwarded it to me. The typing frequently went careering off the page, there were beer stains and repetitions but you'd hardly read five pages before you recognised a great entertainer."

The tattered bundle, replete with tell-tale stains and missing lines, was "The Quare Fellow", a play about the execution of a prisoner in Mountjoy Jail in Dublin, based on an actual event that took place during one of Behan's stays there. This was also the play that had launched him on the world when the Pike Theatre in Dublin staged it for the first time in 1954. Two years down the line, Littlewood realised its wider potential immediately. She was so impressed she sent him his fare to come to London at once to discuss putting it on at her space in the East End.

Behan drank the money. So she sent more. He drank that too. The third time proved a charm. He arrived in Stratford and so began a relationship that was to serve them both very well for the next few years. Behan deserved and wanted a wider audience and Theatre Workshop needed a money-spinning and headline-grabbing production that would impact beyond their small coterie of faithful supporters. "The Quare Fellow" opened on May 24th, 1956, and it proved to be a break-out play for them both.

"It is Ireland's sacred duty to send over every few years a playwright who will save the English theatre from inarticulate dumbness," wrote Kenneth Tynan, the most influential British critic of his generation, in The Observer. "And Irish dialogue almost invariably sparkles."

With plenty more gushing reviews of that ilk, the show wasn't long for Stratford. Just eight weeks later, it moved to the West End. The critical reaction to the work soon placed Behan in the company of an emerging generation of daring, innovative dramatists like John Osborne and Shelagh Delaney. Perhaps the biggest triumph of all this was that, in Littlewood, he had happened upon somebody with the patience to tolerate his erratic work practices and the ability to improve his writing for the stage.

"Joan Littlewood suited my requirements exactly," wrote Behan. "She has the same views on the theatre that I have, which is that the music hall is the thing to aim at for to amuse people and any time they get bored, divert them with a song or a dance. I've always thought T. S. Eliot wasn't far wrong when he said that the main problem of the dramatist today was to keep his audience amused; and that while they were laughing their heads off, you could be up to any bloody thing behind their backs; and it was what you were doing behind their bloody backs that made your play great."

The box office was helped immeasurably by Behan's performance during a television interview with Malcolm Muggeridge on the BBC. After a day's drinking, he turned up to the studio in a state of disrepair that ensured he went down in history as the first man to appear drunk on British television. His display appalled some but delighted many of those watching at home, unused to seeing such unfiltered reality on their screens. Whether they liked or loathed a broadcast that culminated in him delivering a very slurred rendition of "The Auld Triangle", they all knew who he was now. In one night in that summer of 1956, he turned from a somewhat-celebrated writer into a national celebrity.

From that point, Behan's star continued to rise until it reached unique heights two years later. In the space of a few weeks in October and November, 1958, a production of "The Quare Fellow" opened and was well-received on Broadway; "Borstal Boy", his memoir of his time in a British young offenders' institution, was published in London to critical raves, and his newest play, "The Hostage", debuted at the Theatre Royal. Originally written in Irish as "An Giall", he had translated it into English, expanding it and hamming up the comic elements at the expense of the original tragedy.

The transformation of the play about a British soldier being held hostage by IRA men in a brothel was not all his own work. After her success in shaping "The Quare Fellow", Littlewood had even more input in ushering this piece from the page to the stage. As the title of her company suggested, she was a believer in workshopping every play, constantly improvising and augmenting the text in rehearsals and even between performances. Behan had provided her with the manuscript so late that "The Hostage" was very much a work in progress until she started tailoring it. How much of this was collaborative and how much her own work remained a moot point.

"Dylan Thomas wrote 'Under Milkwood' and Brendan wrote 'under Littlewood'," said the artist Tom Nisbet, summing up what became the commonly-held belief that the director actually wrote more of the play than Behan.

"Without Littlewood, you wouldn't be who and what you are," a jealous author once said to Behan.

"Maybe not," replied Behan. "but, without me, Littlewood wouldn't be who and what she is either."

That much was definitely true. As for how much was written by whom, the most definitive investigation to date was carried out by Dr. David Clare of the NUI, Galway.

"When Behan, as legend has it, wrote the added scenes on stray bits of scrap paper or phoned them in to Littlewood and Raffles from the pub, he obviously, under the pressure of writing to the deadline of the opening night of "The Hostage", relied on good lines and little anecdotes that had already met with success in the pieces of writing he had done for smaller Irish audiences..." wrote Clare. "While this may be 'lazy', it is clear that the accusation that 'Behan's plays were... written for him' (made initially by the poet and playwright Donagh McDonagh and echoed by others) is completely fantastical. Littlewood certainly made cuts to what Behan wrote and rearranged the order of certain scenes, but this is quite common in transferring a play from page to stage."

The disputed authorship may have been the stuff of pub gossip and the future subject of academic speculation but, in September, 1960, it scarcely mattered much. How could it when their collaboration had brought them all the way across the ocean to New York, to the Great White Way? Just four years after unravelling that first fortuitous package from Behan, Littlewood and Raffles had arrived in America ahead of the playwright and their company in order to lay the groundwork for their first show on the biggest stage of all.

"Brendan has a gutsy humorous viewpoint about everything – even death," said Littlewood in an interview with the New York Times. "He has his serious side but he's a great clown. He's not publicly searching his soul like some playwrights, but trying to find some fun out of life. It's the key to his popularity."

Caroline Burke Swann and Leonard Field, this pair of veteran New York producers, had been so taken with the quality of production they'd witnessed in London that they battled with both US Immigration and Actor's Equity to ensure almost the entire cast and crew were brought across to replicate those performances at the Cort Theatre on West 48th Street. If that meant the players were very comfortable with the material, there were still problems to be surmounted. The stage manager objected to a scene where the American flag is allowed fall to the floor and Littlewood herself was appalled by the set that had been built. She demanded it be made over into a less gloomy and less Celtic affair.

During the course of this transformation, somebody painted the slogan "God Bless Our Home" on one of the walls of the brothel. Swann wondered aloud whether a more specifically Irish slogan might be used to add flavour. Behan considered the point and then suggested they might use the Irish translation of "God Bless Our Home", which he assured her was, "Pog Mo Thoin". Swann was delighted and put the prop man to work immediately. The new wording was soon there for all to see. That was when the co-producer noticed every Irish person in the room giggling and laughing and pointing. Then somebody translated its true meaning for her benefit; Kiss My Ass.

Part of the play's original charm was how contemporary so many references were. This required more changing of the text between London and New York. Behan and Littlewood were determined to continue inserting local allusions into the play as well, boasting to reporters shortly after arriving that they'd already added a crowd-pleasing line about how fond President Dwight Eisenhower was of golf. Coming to the end of his second term in office, Eisenhower had reputedly played 800 rounds while at the White House.

In his pursuit of this type of relevance, Behan brought lines he'd picked up on the streets or in Manhattan bars, obviously finding pubs fertile ground now that he was sober enough to remember the best gags delivered in them. The actors and actresses were also encouraged to pour over the papers each morning in the search for suitable material that might be worked into the text. Always, they had to be careful not to step over the line into vulgarity. For all Behan's crudity on and off the page, Littlewood felt he had a certain way of doing things that was pitched just perfectly.

"If the contacts in the play become heavy or lecherous for the sake of lechery, they will be repulsive to the audience," she said. "There is no lechery in Behan; all his lavatory doors have little hearts cut in them."

If Littlewood loved the fact the play changed almost every night, drawing special glee from the fact Behan could be pro-something one day and anti-it the next, everybody was too busy enjoying the ride to catalogue all the changes made to the text. "He never bothered about what was written down, the tragic thing is somebody wrote down a very bad travesty of it after," said Littlewood.

For her part, as a producer, Swann had never seen anything quite like the way they worked. Still, she quickly became a fan of their rather unorthodox approach.

"Patience Collier (Miss Gilchrist) brought in an item which she wanted to use," wrote Swann. "It described Queen Elizabeth's and the Duke of Edinburgh's tiger hunt in India, emphasising the queen's costume and the duke's bagging of a tiger. It was immediately included, plus Brendan's ad-libbed verse:

Tiger, tiger, burning bright
In the forest of the night
Tell me, was it just a fluke
You got potted by the Duke?

While all this was going on in preparation for the opening night, Behan continued to impress in cameos around town. One afternoon, Field brought him to lunch with the novelist John Cheever at Sardi's on 44th Street, the place to see or be seen for anybody involved in Broadway. Field and Cheever traced their friendship back nearly two decades to when they served together in the Signal Corps of the US Army. Cheever didn't know too much about "The Hostage" at this point but immediately deduced from the way that people were making a fuss of the Irishman, signs were everybody expected the play to do well.

"We had lunch with Behan," wrote Cheever, "and I'm sure the show will be a great success because why otherwise should Vincent (Sardi Jr – owner of the restaurant) come to the table practically on his hands and knees and why should Lennie Lyons (the gossip columnist) embrace me?"

If the bold-faced names of New York society were fussing over Behan in a way that was apparent to as keen an observer as Cheever, a novelist regarded by one critic as "the Chekov of the suburbs," Behan was still having assimilation problems.

"What the fuck is this fucking cannelloni?" he roared upon receiving the meal he'd ordered that day. After some hasty consultation, a second version of the dish was produced, this time containing chicken. Again, Cheever read much into the restaurant catering for the big star's every whim and, though envious, it was a remark that spoke to the dazzling wattage of Behan's celebrity in those opening few weeks in America.

As diligent Littlewood continued to hone the play, Behan had enough time on his hands to be driven up to Cheever's home in Scarborough on the Hudson River by Ginnie Field, Leonard's wife.

"I recall [him] as hugely jolly and hugely fat," wrote Cheever's son Benjamin. "He was wearing swimming trunks when I met him and had a cigar in his mouth and a navel that seemed almost as black and stuck out as far as the cigar."

Benjamin's older sister remembered Behan singing to her: "The bells of hell go ting a ling a ling for you but not for me, O death where is thy sting a ling a ling, O grave thy victory." Ever the egotist, he couldn't help giving her the song sung by the corpse of the British soldier at the end of "The Hostage". If the purpose of his run to the country was to allow Behan to indulge his love of swimming, he, of course, left more of an impression than just the children marveling at the size of his belly and the beauty of his voice.

"Now that I'm off the sauce – he said – I'm much more interested in farney," wrote Cheever of another cameo from this encounter. "What is farney – asked Mrs. Vanderlip (who owned the house Cheever rented). 'Farney, Mam,' said Behan, 'is an abbreviation for farnacation.' I like him tremendously and I'm sure the play will be a great success."

On September 19th, the night before the play was due to open, Behan drank a quart of seltzer at Lawton Carver's, a restaurant near the United Nations. Although the city was filling up with heads of state from all over the planet ahead of the General Assembly in that very building, his sighting and his drink of choice was thought worthy of mention in the following morning's gossip columns.

The same day's papers contained a snippet about him turning up at a party and doing a turn. He assured the guests at the shindig that "acting is harder than working in a tunnel under the river." Then he sang three songs and before leaving, quipped, "Well, as we say on the Northern border, 'see you later detonator' or 'later tonight dynamite'."

CHAPTER FOUR

A Night To Remember

Yet Brendan had arrived in triumph, and I wondered if I were unduly possessive, like a mother anxious to protect her child from a harsh world. I loved my husband as he was now, clean, healthy, glowing from the shower. Liquor coarsened him and saddened me. I feared that in the end it would destroy the intimacy between us.

BEATRICE BEHAN

ON the morning of September 20th, 1960, the front pages of newspapers across America were dominated by the impending opening of the 15th Session of the United Nations General Assembly in New York. All of the world's leaders had descended on New York City. Up at the Hotel Theresa in Harlem, the Soviet leader Nikita Krushchev met and, later, famously hugged Cuba's Fidel Castro, even as those protesting his visit clashed with police on Park Avenue. Out on the campaign trail, the presidential candidates, Richard Nixon and John F. Kennedy, both referenced the significance of the presence of the USSR's bogeyman on American soil in speeches that day.

If there was serious stuff afoot then, on the inside pages, several dozen newspapers around the country also carried a syndicated Associated Press interview with Beatrice Behan, beneath a range of colourful headlines such as, "Brendan Behan's wife isn't meek, mousy type of spouse" and "Married a Sot and she's happy!"

"Yes there is a Mrs. Brendan Behan," wrote Joe Miller, introducing middle America to the woman behind the man. "But she's not the mousy little woman you might expect to be married to a roaring Irishman like the playwright of "The Hostage". Beatrice Behan is a slim, dark-haired girl with a twinkle in her gray-blue eyes and an easy manner that's sometimes devastating in its matter-of-factness. She is as off-hand about her husband's past peccadilloes as she is unimpressed by the flurry over his play opening tonight on Broadway."

In an interview, where she held forth, amongst other things, on the impressive modern architecture of the city, the helpfulness of the taxi-drivers, and the quality of the "feminine make-up", Beatrice also recounted the story of when she first met Brendan. Her father, the artist Cecil ffrench-Salkeld, had brought a stranger back from a pub to the family home on Morehampton Road in Donnybrook, Dublin following a drinking spree. All she remembered of that first encounter was that the young visitor wore a moustache, a charge he later denied. For his part, Behan always claimed Beatrice had been "impolite" to him that night. In any case, their paths crossed again years later and to better effect.

"He took me to the races in December," she said. "We were married in February, 1955."

A brief summation of what was a brief courtship and a whirlwind romance. It had culminated in a very private wedding, with a dozen people, none from his family, in attendance at 7am in Donnybrook Church. Like so much else about their relationship, the formalities of it had been unconventional, as was much of it thereafter.

"It's a happy marriage," Beatrice told Miller. "We've had our ups and downs but everyone has that, life's very agreeable, very entertaining. Of course he gets excited over things and sometimes I get the backwash of it. I understand that. He always says later he's sorry, that he has to let off steam."

A disturbing description of any relationship yet Miller

didn't delve deep enough to ask exactly what constituted "backwash". Instead, he was more impressed that, as he recited the litany of Behan misadventures through the years from his notes, Beatrice simply explained away each offence as him having "too much of the gargle". There were other questions too. She was asked her view of American women.

"I think they're very kind. I've always heard this is a woman's country, that women dominated men. But I haven't seen any sign of it. If anything it's the other way around. Except the other day at the beach, right after we came. A woman with us asked Brendan to carry the picnic basket. He handed it to me. She said, 'Oh no, he's supposed to carry it; he's a man.' Brendan was horrified."

If that anecdote offered a revealing insight into Behan's attitude towards his wife, she never forgot the purpose of the interview, remembering to plug the show.

"It's a terribly entertaining play," said Beatrice. "The English loved it, in spite of the digs. Americans will get a few digs too, we'll see how they like it."

To the outside observers who spotted him in the lobby of the Algonquin Hotel that afternoon, Behan did not have the outward complexion of a man overly concerned with how the play was going to be received. In suitably gregarious form, he received very public phone calls of congratulations from various people, and took time out to write a postcard to his friend James McKenna whose play "The Scatterin'" had just opened in Dublin. A magnanimous gesture from a man counting down the hours to the biggest night of his own career.

Of course, Behan had already outlined his strategy for dealing with the pressures of opening a play on Broadway.

"Now if you get six out of six good reviews, you can ask the President of the United States to sell you the White House, though I don't think this has ever happened. If you get five good reviews, you are doing fairly well, and you have to start worrying about 480 Lexington Avenue, which is the home of the income tax. It is not a bad kind of worry in its own way, if you have got to have worries, and I suppose everyone has to have them.

"If you have four you can afford to give a party, or at least you can afford to attend the party which is usually given for you. If you get three good reviews, it's time like to go home to bed, but if you only get two, you sit there the whole of the following day and don't go out until after dark. If you get one good review, you must make an air reservation very quickly, to get back to where you came from, but if you get six bad reviews you take a sleeping pill. You might even take an overdose."

The walk from the hotel to the Cort Theatre should, at the most leisurely pace, take no more than ten minutes. However, in typical fashion, Behan, wearing a crumpled blue suit, was late to the show that night, his tardiness not helped by him dawdling outside the doors, "holding court" with his fans as one observer put it. Inside, the producers growing ever so slightly agitated held the curtain in anticipation of him finally reaching his seat in the mezzanine. The delay meant that the play didn't finish until 11pm, something that gave the critics just 30 minutes in which to write and phone in their reviews on deadline afterwards.

"It deserved a well-considered reaction," wrote Howard Taubman, New York's most-feared critic years later. "An hour of writing time would not have been amiss."

They coveted the extra time because, like it or not, this was no ordinary play. If nothing else, it stretched the parameters.

"Have you got the place well-covered sir?" asked Mr. Pat (Max Shaw) early in the second act.

"I have indeed, why?" replied the IRA officer (Victor Spinetti)

"I think it's going to rain," said Mr. Pat.

The crowd laughed heartily and, buoyed by their reaction, Spinetti swung around to face them, put his hand in the air and shouted: "Silence! This is a serious play!"

They loved that even more.

"I didn't do it to show off," wrote Spinetti. "It wasn't an ad lib I'd worked out before going on. I was simply, in that moment, an IRA officer on my platform. The next day the papers said: 'Brendan Behan flings up his hand and commands Broadway to silence.' The phone rang. It was Brendan."

Any actor might have feared hearing from the playwright the morning after an impromptu cameo of that ilk. But Behan was a very different animal when it came to the sacredness of the text.

"Vic," he said, "that line you put in last night. Keep it in. It's one of the funniest fuckin' lines I never wrote."

There was more improv too. At an another juncture, somebody in the crowd roared up, "Are you really having a ball up there?"

"Sure, come and join us," quipped Spinetti.

He didn't miss a beat. None of them did. This interaction was all part of the cabaret.

"We were used to interruptions; at Stratford, we'd encouraged them, enjoyed them and hoped the same thing would happen in New York," wrote Littlewood. "It did."

Surprisingly, and perhaps disappointingly for some given his reputation, the one person who kept schtum throughout the production was Behan himself. His unscheduled and often chaotic interruptions had become part of the fabric on the London stage. Here, on a night when Beatrice noticed he was especially nervous sitting in his seat, he stayed true to his promise to keep out of the action. When reporters caught him during the intermission however, he was in the mood to chat.

"If it's a flop, New York has lost a playwright and gained a tourist," said Behan. "If it's a success, I imagine we'll join the queue looking for an apartment. I'll stay here for a few months to count the people coming in. I'm a very suspicious man."

At the finish, the crowd were on their feet, giving an ovation. One report tallied the number of curtain calls at ten. An impromptu chant of "author, author" went up, and Behan, after a fashion, responded, by rising from his seat to mumble a few phrases that were difficult for many people to hear and for the rest to understand. For once, perhaps overcome by the enormity of the occasion, he was, kind of, lost for words.

As is usual on opening night, the drama was only beginning. While the critics went away to file reviews which everybody, as per tradition, now eagerly awaited, the Behans headed for the after-party. It was a two-legged affair. First, there was a stop at Sardi's where, as was customary with every premiere, the rest of the diners rose to toast "The Hostage" party with champagne. Brendan found the atmosphere there too boring for his liking so they moved on to Jim Downey's Restaurant on 44th Street, where the host had commissioned a cake with a bust of Behan's head on the icing.

Much more his kind of joint, this was the place where Behan's old and new lives intersected that night, with predictably amusing results. Freddy Boland had missed the play but he made it to the celebrations and he came bearing quite the excuse to explain his absence. Ireland's Ambassador to the General Assembly, Boland had been delayed at the office due to the number of nations wanting to speak about the admission of new members.

"Your show went well, I see," said the bespectacled Boland as he greeted Behan. "Come to that, my own show went well. I was elected President of the United Nations."

The pair had uniquely Dublinesque history. Behan had first

met Boland's wife Frances Kelly, an artist, when she was doing a mural at the Bakers' Union offices in Gardiner Street at the same time as he was painting the walls there. If Boland's new-found celebrity (the Communist nations at the UN had refused to applaud his election) ensured his presence at the party made the newspapers the next day, it also irked some of Behan's knockers.

"Mr. Freddy Boland, and the entire Irish delegation came…" said Behan. "This greatly upset the New York Irish middle classes. The recent Irish arrivals there of the past forty years — those who had made money but were still born in Ireland — were kind of upset. Well, they didn't know what to do. They thought that, of course, if I was good enough for a cabinet minister, then I must be OK. It might seem as if I was accepted."

While stars like Lauren Bacall and her boyfriend and future husband, Jason Robards Jr, were in attendance too, all of course paled next to Jackie Gleason, then starring at the Shubert Theatre in "Take Me Along". The comic wasn't going to miss the first night festivities for the man he'd found so hilarious, unintentionally or otherwise, on Edward R. Murrow's "Small World" the previous year. Gleason was also the man who caught the eye of Behan's uncle that night.

Jimmy Kearney had emigrated to America after World War 1 and became an elevator operator at the headquarters of Chase Manhattan Bank just off Wall Street. The young Brendan remembered dollars being sent back to Dublin by his uncle even during the darkest years of the Depression. Having him in the same room as Gleason this night then was a neat way to pay back his uncle, and Behan noted that Jimmy and his wife Kathleen were much more interested in shaking the comic's hand than celebrating Boland's political and diplomatic triumph on the world stage.

According to Behan, "They wanted to tell my little cousin Margaret that they had spoken to Jackie Gleason which apparently was like having an audience with the Pope."

The "Pope" was in especially uproarious form that night, seemingly determined to make merry with his new pal from Ireland. Indeed, one eyewitness recalled Gleason unceremoniously shoving Boland (a man at the centre of a geopolitical storm that was worrying the world) out of the way in order to get to Behan.

"Come on," said Gleason, at one point. "Let's talk Irish!"

"Where the hell did you learn Irish?" asked Behan.

"Oh I can count up to ten," said Gleason, a man who himself had a love affair with drink.

"Conas atá tú?" asked Behan, figuring that if his fast friend knew any cupla focal, it would be the most basic greeting.

"One, two, three, four," replied Gleason smiling.

The type of inane joke that somebody who is drunk finds hilarious. The sort of rubbish that Behan himself had visited on hundreds of people over the years. The shoe was on the other foot in Downey's though because Gleason had been drinking hard and Behan was stone cold sober. Malachy McCourt was present that evening, a professional actor who regarded "The Hostage" causing such a kerfuffle as "a triumphant night for the Irish". He also witnessed the kind of pressure Gleason put on Behan to get drunk with him.

"Jackie Gleason was uproariously sizzled and trying to get Brendan to start on the sauce," wrote McCourt. "People kept telling Gleason to lay off, but he persisted until he got so out of hand we had to eject the Great One onto the sidewalks of New York and lock the door behind him. It was a bizarre sight, watching him leaping and hopping like one of those balloons in the Macy's Thanksgiving Day Parade, shaking his pudgy fists, the face contorted with what we presumed were curses and imprecations flowing out of the face hole, as we could hear nothing with the door being closed."

The unfortunate Gleason cameo didn't detract from the event or distract Behan from his sobriety. With Beatrice drinking soda in solidarity with his own efforts, he stayed away from alcohol and the party continued without the most famous comedian in America.

"Every actor had a pretty girl on each arm, each actress an attentive lad, or one or two or three or more," recalled Joan Littlewood. "When those Broadway babies said good night, it was tomorrow morning and the wage slaves were hurrying along the sweaty streets."

By that stage in the festivities, the Behans were long gone. As the party went on, Beatrice had grown concerned about her husband's ability to resist this much alcoholic temptation so they'd left for a quieter gathering with a pair of old friends, Oonagh, Lady Oranmore and Browne, one of the heirs to the Guinness fortune, and her son Garech.

They found a bar on 52nd Street where, at Garech's insistence, Brendan, still perfectly sober, belted out songs. On a number of different levels, the night had gone well. It remained only for the newspapers to pass judgment.

"The reviews were all right," said Behan, "they weren't quite as good as London but they were civil."

Some of them were more than civil, others less.

In the New York Daily News, John Chapman called Behan "Ireland's one-man answer to the Katzenhammer Kids", a reference to a slapstick cartoon strip that was popular at the time. Chapman didn't mean it as a compliment. While admitting parts of the show were funny, he described Behan's knowledge of stage craft as "primitive" and accused him of tossing "everything into a theatrical mulligatawny which lacks the tang of a soundly-made Irish stew". He went on to question the originality of the piece and to point out that several of the jokes were old and hackneyed.

In The New York Herald Tribune, Walter Kerr jnr was kinder.

"In dashing all of this off at breakneck speed, Mr. Behan is three or four persons at once," wrote Kerr. "He is a kind of infant exhibitionist, proud of his never having been trained (the number of calculated shockers and his may well be the play with something to offend everybody, not always to the good of the occasion.) He is a random humorist, ready to borrow from absolutely anyone ("I'm as pure as the driven snow: You weren't driven far enough"). He is again a better humorist than that, an original piece of salt who may remind you of Mort Sahl or the more extravagant Mark Twain, or just of your drunken uncle who happened to be a true wit."

If the Kerr comparisons with Sahl (a popular comedian of the time) and the iconic Twain were positive, the critic who carried most weight in the city was Taubman of the New York Times. The headline over his piece the following morning read "Behan Buffoonery", a phrase that could be interpreted as positive or negative, it perfectly suited what he wrote. Taubman dished out some lavish praise at the same time as he poured scorn on some aspects of a production he felt "mixes irreverent hilarity with tasteless rubbish".

"The evening is like a wild one in combination saloon and bawdy house," wrote Taubman. "The inmates are capable of richly amusing observations and unalleviated dullness. They sing and dance and have fun, occasionally sharing that precious commodity with the public. Vive le sport! Mr. Behan is a man of immense talent but in 'The Hostage', he seems to spew on it more often than use it with purpose. If he were really not serious about anything, he might be excused for being so cavalier with his gifts. But even in this undisciplined invention, he reveals a flair for drama and a determination to communicate something."

In the end, Taubman, who legendarily possessed the power to close a show with a harsh review, advised his readers: "If you are willing to shuttle madly between delight and distaste, you might try dancing to Mr. Behan's Irish jig."

Plenty of people were willing to take Taubman's advice.

"I believe we've got a hit," said Leonard Field, citing a box office of $24,353 in the opening week despite losing some custom to the Jewish holidays. "It's coming along very nicely."

If that's exactly what you'd expect the producer of a play to say to a reporter, the numbers backed him up. The maximum they could have done in that time frame was $35,000 so the returns were at the very least respectable. Not to mention too that after a modest advance sale, Field said window sales had been improving every night. The fact four out of the six main reviews were positive obviously had helped too. In any case, Behan wasn't holding any grudges.

One afternoon, he met Henry Hewes, drama critic of the Saturday Review, on the street near the Algonquin.

"You know of course that I gave your show a bad notice," said Hewes.

"That's all right," said Behan, "let's go and have a drink."

They went into a bar where Behan ordered a soda water and Hewes had a high ball (bourbon whiskey, ginger ale and a twist of lemon). As they sat there shooting the breeze, some cast members from "The Hostage" happened to walk in, recognised the critic sitting at the table and did a double-take.

"It's okay," said Behan, "I'm consoling Henry for the bad review he gave our play."

CHAPTER FIVE

The Wheels Come Off The Wagon

I suspect Behan's public displays are closely tied to the state of his box office. Behan is an Irish 'Uncle Tom'. Negro performers use Uncle Tom as a contemptuous description of coloured actors who are over humble, self-serving caricatures of the negro who doesn't read and talks a funny mush-mouth southern-accented drivel. Mr. Behan is a caricature of the drunken Irishman. I would happily accept his problem as none of my affair if he would just once get a spontaneous load on and forget to play 'Paddy the Mick' who hates the English and roars 'Up the IRA.' I am as Irish as Mr. Behan and I resent his contrived and profitable playing of an old stereotype character, the drunken Irishman.

BILL SLOCUM, NEW YORK JOURNAL AMERICAN, NOVEMBER, 1960

ON October 7th, Behan was invited to give a guest lecture at Vassar, a liberal arts college then restricted to women students, located in the Hudson Valley town of Poughkeepsie, a couple of hours up the river from New York. One of the so-called Seven Sisters colleges, established as the distaff equivalent of the Ivy League institutions, the man now being dubbed "the Irish Lenny Bruce" by some New York reporters was so taken by his surroundings that he later described the university as his "Tír Na nÓg".

On campus, his itinerary included sitting in on a class (with surprising little interruptions), a private supper with selected faculty and then the speech at the college's experimental theatre. If those present were expecting a formal lecture, what they got was more freeform poetry slam, part stand-up comedy, part theatrical improv, all entertainment.

"On Thursday evening, a tubby Irishman in a crumpled green suit climbed the steps in Avery and delivered an outlandish, unrehearsed performance, which, in this reviewer's opinion, has never been surpassed at Vassar," wrote Diana Fries in The Vassar Miscellany News. "Puffing mightily on an aromatic cigar, Mr. Behan rambled on about Vassar girls, chorus girls. Irish orphanages, Americans abroad, to mention only a few of the topics he covered. It would be impossible to recapture what Mr. Behan talked about to his audience of 'faculty members, madonnas and escorts'."

Behan brought his audience on a trip through his life, personal and professional, switching between accents to better deliver each anecdote. One minute, impersonating a New York producer, the next recounting the difficulties a drunk Dublin actor faced when playing the French emperor. The crowd loved it. "I suffer from agoraphobia," he told them, "fear of agriculture". An old line, used many times before, but to the naïve undergraduates, even his well-worn material (there are only two theatres in Dublin – Sodom and Begorrah!) was all new and fresh and guaranteed to outrage and delight idealistic and mostly wealthy young women bent on one day changing the world.

"People who say manual labour is a good thing have never done any," said Behan, mixing in a little social commentary with the comic relief. The students loved a routine in which he held forth on the way Americans conduct themselves when visiting Ireland. And amazingly, through all this, he never strayed over the line with any of his gags. Whether it was his sobriety, or his desire not to offend a largely female audience, he never dipped into the bottomless well of vulgar material at his disposal.

"Several things stood out about this man who speaks 'Irish,

English, and rubbish'; one was his unaffected attitude which enabled him to extemporise at will," wrote Fries. "Another was that Behan, whether he is an important new Irish writer or not, is obviously a perceptive spectator with the ability to capture exactly what is amusing about people and things. This last, combined with his gift for mime, allowed his Vassar audience a glimpse into his world, one filled with laughter and disillusionment. Brendan Behan was funny, witty, and vital. His talk, despite its disorganisation, covered a great deal of ground and informed his audience of his opinions about people and things in the world as well as in Ireland."

This version of Behan, impressive, kind of erudite and always engaging was on show for a larger audience three nights later when he was a guest on NBC's Tonight show. With Arlene Francis sitting in as guest host for the absent Jack Paar, Behan featured alongside the actress Constance Cummings, and the comedy duo Jack Burns and George Carlin (who would go on to become arguably the greatest and most subversive stand-up of his generation). The programme commanded such an audience that, pretty soon, Beatrice noticed more and more people recognising and engaging with Brendan on the streets of New York.

Next up on the playwright of the moment's packed schedule was an even more eclectic venue, the Young Men's Hebrew Association on 92nd Street, where he had been booked to read from his works and to discuss contemporary theatre.

"The Hebrews and the Gaels have much in common," Behan told his audience. "Both are exotic enough to be interesting, and foreign enough to be alarming."

Leonard Lyons, the gossip columnist and somebody fast becoming his good friend, accompanied Behan to that gig. Afterwards, the pair of them repaired to Chez Vito, a fashionable supper club on 60th Street near Madison Avenue. When the violinists on duty recognised Behan in their midst, they deviated from their usual repertoire to play "Danny Boy" and then "Mother Machree". Of course, the moment he heard a familiar note being struck, Behan immediately sang along with gusto. Then, he ordered champagne for the musicians while sticking strictly to the club soda himself.

Manus Canning arrived in New York at this time. He had never met Behan before but they had mutual friends and the IRA in common. Canning had barely touched down when he received a phone call from Behan, mentioning his pal Cathal Goulding (with whom Manning had served time in prison), and inviting the new arrival to spend a day with him at Aqueduct Racetrack, near Idlewild Airport. The friendship grew from there and, as he accompanied the Dubliner around the city, Canning saw how comfortable he was in the new surroundings. This was Behan and New York city during the extended honeymoon period.

"I think that was the high point of Brendan's life for pleasure here. It was a very warm and pleasant thing to walk around New York with him at that time," said Canning. "He made it feel like a small town. This was perhaps one kind of greatness that his humanity came out. He knew the cops in the street; he knew their names, they knew him. The doorman, the waiters, everybody knew Brendan and he could quite often come up with their names and slap their back, shake their hands, and as I say, it gave a pleasant feeling of being in a small town. He made New York feel like a small town at that time."

It was a measure of his growing celebrity that Behan's mere presence in the Algonquin was being noted too by so many. Harper Lee, whose book "To Kill a Mocking-Bird" had just been released, was sitting in the lobby of the hotel one afternoon, being interviewed by a reporter from Newsweek, when Behan came barging in. She immediately recognised him and told the journalist excitedly: "I've always wanted to meet an author." Obviously, this was before Lee herself became something of a recluse.

Behan was meeting plenty of literary luminaries himself. Shortly after the play opened, he was introduced to Allen Ginsberg, darling poet of the Beat Generation, counter-cultural icon and somebody Behan described as "a very interesting and important man". They posed for the portrait photographer Richard Avedon. Beatrice and Peter Orlovsky, Ginsberg's life partner looking on as Brendan, wielding a fat cigar, leans across to hear Ginsberg make a point.

"He was full of energy and inquisitiveness," said Ginsberg. "He came down to our apartment on the Lower East Side and we sat around the kitchen talking. He liked poetry. We talked about Yeats, talked about Irish poetry. I was broke actually so he offered to take us out, down to Delancey Street to the Romanian Jewish restaurants for eats. So all four of us went down.

"The thing I remember most vividly is towards the end of the meal, I went downstairs to the men's room and he got up from the table and followed me. He stopped me in the hall outside the toilet and said, 'Have you got any ammunition?' 'Ammunition?' 'Money.' I said, 'No.' So he took out a wad of bills and he gave me about $80. He had no reason to do that, except he was open-hearted and I guess he was making money on his play."

On another occasion, John Simon, theatre critic with New York magazine, caught a glimpse of Behan's obsessive dislike of dining alone.

"The one time I met Brendan Behan, a bunch of us were sitting in the Algonquin lobby, fairly late, when somebody – the waiter or his keeper – came up and asked whether we would kindly keep Mr. Behan company while he ate his dinner," wrote

Simon. "Apparently, this helped him eat, just as his witty and variously informed conversation helped us down our nightcaps. He twitted us all with that bellicose charm of his, and I still cherish the oxymoron of 'Balkan Metternich' which he coined for me."

As the flavour of the month or indeed of that whole season, there were constant invitations to events and umpteen requests for audiences with the new kid in town. If the excitement and glamour of those first few weeks in New York perhaps served to distract Behan from his thirst for drink, those closest to him were growing concerned that the pace might prove too hectic. The feeling was that his desire to enjoy his new status and to maximise this extraordinary, career-defining and life-changing opportunity might prove detrimental to his health.

At the Algonquin one night, Beatrice and her sister Celia had a conversation in which both expressed to each other exactly how worried they had become that life in the fast lane might derail him. Gerry Raffles also suggested to Beatrice it might be smart for Behan to get out of New York sooner rather than later. More than once, Beatrice thought of raising the issue with Behan as they lay in bed in the morning discussing their latest adventures in the city that never sleeps. But, knowing her husband better than anybody, she feared the very act of advising him to ease off on his engagements would most likely have the opposite effect.

In a matter of weeks, he'd become part of the furniture at the Algonquin. Harry Celentano, who worked the elevators, recalled Behan coming downstairs in his pyjamas one morning, heading for his breakfast until the dining room captain intercepted him and pointed out he was improperly dressed for the meal. Never at a loss for words, Behan turned and asked the captain if he'd worn pyjamas while having his breakfast.

"Ah yes, Mr. Behan, but I ate at home," said the captain.

"Well, this is my home now!" said Behan, before marching towards the nearest coffee pot.

Living at such a prestigious address suited him. As he often told interviewers, he liked to live well. Amongst other things, he developed a fondness for Hauptmann cigars that he purchased at Dunhill's on Fifth Avenue.

"And even before I ever saw Dunhill's, I was still fond of a good cigar and you don't exactly find them growing on trees up in the Phoenix Park," Behan told one interviewer.

It behoved a man to dress appropriate to his newfound station. He did this too, after a fashion, claiming, "A typical Behan costume is a Brooks Brothers suit with two buttons off and a big fucking booze stain on the front."

By October, 1960 Brooks Brothers had already been in business in New York for nearly a century and a half. Headquartered on Madison Avenue, their status as America's oldest men's clothier made them the preferred choice of the rich and the powerful. Famously, President Abraham Lincoln had been wearing one of their coats when he was assassinated by John Wilkes Booth at the Ford Theatre in Washington. Behan wasn't long in town when he made the first of many stops at the Brooks Brothers emporium on Manhattan's most fashionable boulevard. His eye was taken by a cashmere coat that looked perfectly suited for the job of keeping him warm as winter drew in.

"How much is it?" he asked.

"Two hundred and eighty dollars," answered the salesman who, earning his corn, had already told Behan his own family hailed from Ireland too, the traditional line of an American shop assistant trying to flog something to an Irish customer. In today's money, the coat was priced at just under $2200. Of course, words not numbers were Behan's forte. He bought the garment without even flinching. It wasn't until he returned to the Algonquin that the reality of the price actually hit home, and, only then with the assistance of others.

When Bob Bennett, an English waiter at the hotel informed him he'd just forked out the equivalent of £100, Behan feigned indifference.

"Well, I can hardly go back now and ask them for something a little more reasonable. I shall just have to impress everyone with it back home in Ireland."

For several months before New York and for 54 days since arriving, Brendan Behan had remained sober. Quite an achievement considering the amount of socialising he was doing, the amount of temptation being placed in his path. He was slavishly sticking to soda water with lime and even though at more than one party, he'd picked up the wrong glass and taken a sip, he immediately spat it out and went back to the water. At the Four Seasons Hotel one night, the bartender placed four glasses on the table and put the bottle of brandy in front of the most famous drinker in the group.

"This is the best way to handle liquor," said Behan as he filled three of the glasses and left his own dry.

Against that impressive background then, bizarrely, it was the cashmere coat from Brooks Brothers that was to prove his undoing.

On October 25th, he was back on the Tonight Show (a sign of how pleased they were with his previous appearance). On this occasion, he featured alongside a young singer-actress named Florence Henderson (later to gain fame as television matriarch Carol Brady), comedian Cliff Arquette and Kokomo Jr, a performing chimp. As the host Jack Paar expected him to do, Behan delivered an entertaining cameo. He sang a song, ostentatiously smoked a cigar and delivered the type of strong opinion they'd booked him to get.

"Occasionally, there's a daycent remark made on the telly,"

said Behan to a television host who was watched by 30 million Americans every week, "but this is only occasionally."

Aside from recycling the old line about being off drink for Lent as well as breadth, he also joshed with Paar about rumours he was engaged in a buttermilk-drinking contest with his new friend Jackie Gleason. Imagine that. His being on the wagon was so well-known across the country that it was a topic for conversation on a show that Americans tuned into at the end of their evening for light entertainment, one more measure of the rapid fame he'd attained.

"We discussed drinking and I commented on the virtues of temperance," wrote Paar. "Brendan complained that his trouble is that he looks drunk even when he is sober – a point that I had to concede. He has wild hair, a broken nose, a torso that seems to be terraced and his teeth, several of which are missing, look like milestones along a winding country road. While we spoke of the evils of drink I mentioned the advice given me by Leo Genn, the actor: 'If it has to be women or drink, take women because drink always leads to women but women don't necessarily lead to drink!'"

There also ensued a discussion about champagne, something Behan, as a former resident of France, was well able to hold forth on. A small detail, it would gain more significance later.

When he woke up on the morning of October 26th then, all seemed well in Behan's world. The box office was ticking over nicely at the Cort Theatre, and his own legend was being amplified on air and in print on an almost daily basis. He was also the owner of one very expensive and impressive coat. And when Beatrice refused to get the overcoat for him that morning, he decided it was time to go back on the drink.

The scene for the tumbling from the wagon was the Monte Rosa restaurant on 48th Street, a place he'd later describe as "a bit of a madhouse". A suitable venue then. When they sat down for a late lunch that day, Behan ordered champagne, a bottle, not a glass. Beatrice was horrified.

"After a few weeks I was lulled into thinking that Brendan would not touch alcohol again," wrote Beatrice. "Gerry (Raffles) and Joan (Littlewood) and the cast agreed with me. Yet when he broke out in that Spanish restaurant... I knew it wasn't just because I had refused to fetch his overcoat."

Whatever the motivation for him wanting to break out, he ignored her desperate attempts to ask him not to. At one point that afternoon, she dropped to her knees in the middle of the Monte Rosa and loudly begged him to reconsider. The more she implored, the more he ignored. In the end, he was so determined to get drunk that he quaffed the champagne from a water tumbler because he couldn't get enough of it into the narrow flute the waiter had provided. His late and very extended lunch consisted of a large helping of spaghetti, washed down by at least seven (or eight according to differing accounts) bottles of champagne. Suitably lubricated, he headed – where else? – for the Cort Theatre.

His first attempt to gain access to the venue was blocked by ushers, instantly wise to his drunken intent. But they could only keep the tide at bay for so long. In the middle of the second act of that night's performance, Behan marched down the aisle, leaned against the footlights and inserted himself directly into the action during the singing of the song "Nobody Loves You Like Yourself".

Then he went to march back up the aisle but started to stumble. At this point, some of the cast, veterans of these types of interruptions and seasoned enough pros to recognise his inebriated condition, got off the stage to come to his assistance. Perhaps believing he was less dangerous in their care than at loose in the crowd, they brought him back up onto the stage where he joined the ensemble for a song.

"Ladies and gentlemen, this is the most wonderful cast that ever lived," said Behan in an impromptu speech from the front of the stage. "I've brought you the finest actors and actresses in the world, and a good play and if you don't believe it, I don't give a damn. I love America! I didn't think I would but I did."

At the finale, he was literally falling about the place. Almost hit by the curtain coming down, he continued shouting: "You're all welcome. Can you hear me? Can you hear me in the mezzanine? How about the balcony?" Getting into the spirit of the performance, the crowd cheered and applauded and laughed, especially when he continued: "We're operating a clean show. Doing the best that we can. I had a falling out with my wife and it lasted all day!"

Behan didn't appear to notice the shemozzle that took place between a photographer and a member of the production crew during his antics.

"Perry Bruskin, the show's stage manager, was arrested for punching photographer Frank Castrol, and smashing his camera when he tried to take a picture of Brendan's off-stage antics," wrote Michael O'Sullivan in his Behan biography. "While Bruskin was appearing in Night Court before Magistrate Morton R. Tollers, Beatrice was hauling Brendan back to The Algonquin. He threw back a few large whiskeys in the lobby and returned with gusto to his old singing, dancing, hollering form."

The following morning, Americans woke up to newspaper headlines such as "Brendan takes a tumble from the wagon!" and "Behan dropped his milk glass!" Predictable and entirely accurate. One man read the accounts of what happened and felt personally culpable for his part in Behan's downfall.

"Although many guests have come on our show in various states of intoxication, only one that I know of went out and got drunk as a result of being on," wrote Jack Paar. "That was

Brendan Behan, the rumpled Irish playwright who is almost as renowned as a tosspot as he is a writer... After my experience with Behan, I swore off giving temperance lectures. My one to him seemed to have driven him to drink."

In a bizarre sequel, Behan rose from his first hangover in nearly seven months and headed down to the Garment Centre for a John F. Kennedy rally being hosted by the ILGWU. On a day when half a million people saw Kennedy swing through New York on the campaign trail, Behan made the short walk to see in person the candidate he'd wholeheartedly endorsed on his arrival at Idlewild back in early September.

"I like the Democratic Party," said Behan. "I like the look of them. They're the sort of fellows you can call to one side and say, 'My brother Nick is in jail.' They would get your brother out of jail, solely to get your vote of course, but at least they would do something."

This day was less about practical politics and more about a presidential hopeful articulating grandiose notions.

"I believe the issues which separate Mr. Nixon and myself are very clear, and they go to the future of every man and woman here, and they go to the future of our country," said Kennedy. "He has chosen in this difficult time to run on a slogan 'We've never had it so good.' I don't run on that slogan. I run on the slogan 'We are going to have to do much better.'"

Standing at the back of the hall, knowing how much havoc he'd just caused in his private and professional life, Behan must have found the speech rather apt.

Not quite two years later, he lost the controversial and expensive cashmere coat when he left it on a train in France.

CHAPTER 6

If I Touch A Star, Will I Twinkle Too?

Dear Mr. Behan,
I know how frantically busy you must be or I would have
approached you sooner. But if there's an interval, I would
love to have soda with you. I loved your play – it's the best
thing that's happened here in donkey's years.
Kindest regards,
Tennessee (Williams)

THERE are different dates given for exactly when Brendan Behan and Jackie Gleason first met each other in the flesh. Some put the initial encounter as early as September 6th. Others go for later that week. All agree that when it happened it was a coming together of like minds and similar personalities.

"Any chance of you falling off the wagon?" asked Gleason.

"Oh, there's every chance," said Behan. "I was given two rules in Dublin before I came here. Not to fall out of the plane coming over, and not to fall off the boat going back."

They got on famously, a point most eloquently demonstrated by a photograph of the pair, arm in arm backstage, in Gleason's dressing-room at the Shubert Theatre.

"Where are you going to sit?" asked Gleason when he learned Behan had come to see him in "Take Me Along" that evening. "There's a scene in the second act you'll like when I come on drunk. I want to play right up to you."

"That's kind of you certainly," said Behan.

Even though he knew it was coming, Behan still laughed uproariously when Gleason came to the front of the stage as promised. Indeed, he guffawed so loud and long, some people took offence.

"Can't you pipe down?" asked a man sitting nearby.

"I didn't realise you spoke English," said Behan, having none of it.

The pair had become fast friends. The joke was that Behan's next play was being written as a vehicle for Gleason, and was going to be called "Girth of a Nation". In fact, Gleason used to speculate about playing Behan in a production about his life.

"Can you imagine the opening scene?" he asked. "I come rolling down the aisle roaring drunk, while my play's being performed onstage.

Behan was equally effusive about his pal. "What I like about Gleason is that there is a certain sadness of truth about his jokes."

The relationship was, apparently, ready to be taken to the next level.

"Irish playwright Brendan Behan and American comedian Jackie Gleason are going to team up as the 'fabulous fatsos of showbusiness'," wrote journalist Jim Gibbins. "Behan is to write plays for Gleason. 'The team will make history as the heaviest partnership in showbusiness,' Gleason's press agent said this week. Gleason, even on his current diet, weighs 18 stone, and Behan is just a few pounds behind him. But this is the least they have in common...They both hate pomp, officialdom and stuffinesss. They're both up from the slums – Behan, the slums of Dublin, Gleason, the slums of Brooklyn."

Gibbins interviewed the pair in Gleason's hotel suite in New York, making several references to their mutual love of alcohol as both offered explanations as to why they were at that particular time, as luck would have it, off the drink. While Gleason mentioned a punishing work schedule as the reason for his abstemiousness (an assertion that he made a lie of with his antics at the after-party on the opening night of "The Hostage"), Behan cited doctor's orders. "It's medical," he said. "Me stomach, you know."

His new pal perhaps best summed up why Behan was on the wagon. "He had a choice," said Gleason, "it was on or in."

In their mutual sobriety that September, they'd happened upon the plan to work together.

"We have shaken hands and drank a glass of milk apiece on it," said Gleason. "We feel we complement each other pretty well – we also compliment each other too, I'll tell you. So Brendan is going to write a string of plays for me, mostly comedies. But I've so many other commitments at the moment that it won't come off immediately – although you have my assurance this is no hazy dream. After all, we're both on milk!"

After more than a decade as one of the biggest stars on American television, as Ralph Kramden in "The Honeymooners" and at the helm of his own variety show, Gleason had wowed Broadway with the Tony-award winning "Take Me Along". The prospect of him and Behan working together seemed like box-office gold in September, 1960. Like so much else that would happen to the Dubliner in America over the next three years though, it would turn out to be a great idea that never got beyond the planning stages. Nothing ever came of the proposed grand partnership.

Still, for a few weeks that autumn, notwithstanding his fall from the wagon, everything seemed possible as Behan bestrode New York, Darling of the in-crowd, he was a sought-after presence at all the best parties and the most glamorous events. When the movie "Sunrise at Campobello" (dealing with Franklin D. Roosevelt's battle with polio) held its premiere at the RKO Palace Theatre on September 28th, he and Beatrice were guests at the after-party hosted by the former New York Governor W. Averell Harriman and his wife Marie at their home.

As Mrs. Harriman showed them around a town house the walls of which were hung with Renoirs, Picassos, Gaugains, and Van Goghs, the Behans loved gazing upon a collection of masterpieces that would later be donated to the National Gallery of Art in Washington DC.

"I hear one of you paints," said Mrs. Harriman,

"I do," said Beatrice.

"I'm a painter too," said Brendan. "I have the proof right here." At which point, he showed a woman who once owned one of the most influential galleries in New York his painters' union card from Dublin. A cameo so brilliant in its juxtaposition of two worlds that it made it into the gossip columns, Behan, in fact, wore his erudition lightly because the art collection was something he could seriously appreciate and talk about in depth.

"It looks as if our hosts have a 'Douanier'," Behan remarked to Beatrice as they gazed upon yet another master work.

"Actually, that painting is not by the person you mentioned," said a woman standing nearby, using a tone that suggested she was about to enjoy correcting him. "It's by a man called Henry Rousseau."

Sharp as a tack, Behan corrected her on her pronunciation, rolling the name around his mouth in a perfect French accent. "You mean Henri Rousseau."

"Oh, is that what they call him," replied the woman, suddenly on the back foot.

"Yes but he is usually known as 'Le Douanier' which is French for customs' officer because that was his profession before he retired to devote his whole time to painting."

The woman moved away but the moment wasn't lost on a nearby waiter who'd witnessed the exchange and loved the snob being taken to school. "Listen Brendan," he said. "I bet that old bitch is going to throw herself down the elevator shaft now."

Despite the odd clash of civilizations then, he was very comfortable in high society, well able to mix it with the rich and the famous. A lot of times, they sought out his company. Following up on the note quoted above that he dropped into the Algonquin, Tennessee Williams invited the Behans and the cast of "The Hostage" to a party at Café Nicholson, a quirky place on 57th Street beloved of the artistic set. It was to prove an awkward occasion. Brendan and Beatrice were invited into a back room for their audience with the playwright while their fellow travellers were kept outside.

For a left-wing acting troupe from London this was never going to be a workable arrangement. When Beatrice went outside to invite her sister and others into the inner sanctum, they found their path blocked by Frankie Merlo, a Navy veteran who was Williams' partner and, on occasions like this, his bodyguard. When Vincent O'Connor, another cast member, tried to push past regardless, Merlo produced a flick knife. Before the situation could deteriorate further, Brendan emerged and he and his cast soon departed the restaurant. Despite the strangeness of that encounter, the two writers somehow got on. Indeed, Williams would tell reporters later that the pair of them were thinking of collaborating on a play together, and Behan would declare, "The state of Tennessee had the good sense to name itself after a great playwright."

A more objective appraisal of their relationship came from Victor Spinetti.

"Tennessee Williams, who already admired the work of Joan (Littlewood), adored 'The Hostage' and more than that, fell madly in love with Brendan," wrote Spinetti. "'You're a good-looking man, Brendan, you know,' he said. 'You really ought to get yourself some teeth.' 'Who needs fockin' teeth?' said Brendan. 'I took them out and threw 'em in the Liffey!' Anyway, he and Tennessee became very close and often went out together, either for dinner or around the bars. 'Vic,' said Brendan, 'whenever I go out with Tennessee you'll have to come with me and translate. I can't understand a fockin' word he's talking about.'"

Around this time, Mia Farrow was a teenage girl with braces on her teeth, staying at the Algonquin Hotel with her mother, the Roscommon-born actress Maureen O'Sullivan.

"Often we ran into Brendan Behan streaming strong, barely intelligible words, poetry, observations, stories and advice," said Farrow. "It was Brendan who bought me my first drink, a brandy Alexander."

Ever before setting foot in New York, it had been one of his expressed ambitions (so eloquently laid out in his encyclical in The New Yorker) to meet "Marilyn Monroe, back and front." Now that he was famous or infamous enough for her to know who he was, he sent her a note, attached to a copy of her movie "The Misfits". It read: "Marilyn Monroe, a credit to the human race, mankind in general and womanhood in particular."

There is no record of whether she replied but there is this. By that point in her troubled life, Monroe's marriage to playwright Arthur Miller was in trouble, and, to the delight of the New York press, she went on several, very public dates with her ex-husband, the New York Yankees' icon Joe DiMaggio. One of their soirees was a trip to the Cort Theatre to see "The Hostage". No greater compliment perhaps.

So, as Behan immersed himself in all that New York had to offer, the play trundled on in the background.

"It's a custom in New York when a production has been running for a certain amount of time, 13 or 15 weeks, a benefit is given for the unemployed actors and the old actors' home," said Jim Downey, the restaurant owner. "It's called the actors' benefit. The greatest performance without doubt that I ever saw, the greatest acceptance by an audience, was Brendan Behan's

Hostage, Normally, at a benefit you get five or six curtain calls, on this night the show went on for an extra 45 minutes. It was the talk of the theatre world in New York city. It was the best curtain call I've seen in New York in 30 years."

Occasionally, the play was visited by the man himself. One night, Behan came trundling in, well-steamed and determined to become part of the action himself. "Sutton's a bloody queen!" he roared at the top of his voice to the bemusement and amusement of the Broadway crowd. Dudley Sutton, playing the camp character of Rio Rita, knew enough about Behan's modus operandi to anticipate something like this might occur during the course of the run so, ever the true professional, he'd even prepared a comeback to the heckle.

"That's Brendan Behan," he told the audience. "And I know his sister Les Behan." They laughed even harder than before. Little wonder those closest to him could see he was mesmerised by his new surroundings.

"He fell in love with New York," wrote Beatrice. "The reasons were obvious. Brendan hated loneliness and the city's neon lights sustained him far into the night. He judged a city by the ease with which he could talk to its people, and New Yorkers stood on no formality. New York was not romantic like Paris: it was not naïve; it was not traditional like London; it was brash. It held out its arms to Brendan and hugged him."

If his often comic brand of irreverence and his willingness to speak his mind on just about any topic endeared him to the media, others felt his coming had a resounding impact on New York itself. Not only did he liven the place up, he bridged the gap between different parts of town.

"New York was dead in those days," said Norman Mailer. "Brendan's Hostage broke the ice. It made the beatnik movement – (Jack) Kerouac, (Allen) Ginsberg, myself and others – respectable up-town. Before Brendan, we were in exile down in the Village. 'The Hostage' was adored because of its outrageousness and its obscenity, and because of Brendan's captivating humour and eloquence. He was an ice-breaker and the times needed an ice-breaker."

There was perhaps no better illustration of the way the city had warmed to him than through the prism of his relationship with Leonard Lyons. It is in the interest of a gossip columnist to foster good relations with colourful characters who may yield easy column inches but there was much more to their coming together than just that.

"Of all the hundreds of friendships my father enjoyed in his lifetime, perhaps the most unusual and unlikely was the one with Brendan Behan," wrote Lyons' son Jeffrey. "A shy, coffee-drinking New York Jew and a loud gregarious Irish Roman Catholic...."

It says much about how they got on that Behan was invited to Lyons' son Douglas's bar mitzvah. Wearing a yamulka that he brought home as a keepsake, Behan danced the Hora alongside the child's godfather, William O. Douglas, then a Justice in the American Supreme Court.

"I believe you're a judge of the American Supreme Court?" said Behan.

"Yeah, that's right," said Douglas, "how did you know?"

"Well, I know you've got very good clothes and obviously you didn't come by them honestly. But on the other hand, I knew you weren't a politician because you looked a little bit too honest."

Described by Time magazine as the most committed civil libertarian ever to sit on the court, and a defender of free speech since his appointment to the bench by Franklin D. Roosevelt in 1939, Douglas found this type of irreverence towards his position hilarious. There was no record of how the cantor reacted though when Behan told him he practised his

Hebrew pronunciation by listening to New York cab drivers clearing their throats.

For the meal, he sat beside Frank Loesser, an Academy Award winning writer and composer, the man behind the music and lyrics of "Guy and Dolls" and "How to Succeed in Business without really trying," Ethel Merman, the actress/singer and Broadway icon, and the playwright Paddy Chayefsky. Again, the calibre of people around the table summed up the circles he was now moving in.

One evening Lyons brought Brendan and Beatrice to Julius Monks' Downstairs club, another legendary Manhattan nightspot. They were, literally, the only patrons there when a folk singer got up to do a turn.

"Ladies and gentlemen," he said, before laughing at the fact the room was, the Lyons party apart, empty.

"That's all right," said Behan. "When Dean Swift spoke in St. Patrick's in Dublin, the only one there was his butler. So Swift began, 'Dearly beloved Patrick.'"

Now more at ease with his situation, the singer laughed and asked the Behans whether they had any requests. Not the type of question to ask a walking musical archive.

"Do you know this one?" asked Behan, before launching into the first verse of a song.

He didn't. So Behan offered up another number. And another. And another. The singer sat there as the customer's voice filled the room. Lyons relished the unpredictable turn the evening had taken.

"The fact that he is a man of rare talent and a true free spirit made the city open its door to him," wrote Lyons. "We'd been together in many places here, in sawdust rooms and elegant rooms, and every one felt brightened by his wit and his innate warmth. Drinks were being served everywhere and he never touched a drop."

As a gossip columnist, it was Lyons' job to stroll around the city's glamour spots and find out who was where doing what with whom. Part of his routine was to swing by the large theatres to hear about any celebrities attending shows. Many evenings, Behan accompanied him on his travels.

"One of the things my father loved to do with Brendan was take him to half a dozen plays in one hour," wrote Jeffrey Lyons. "My father had the cachet to enter any theatre, unannounced. He and Brendan would stand outside while my father looked at his wristwatch and said something like, 'Okay, it's 9.15, here's the premise of Fiddler on the Roof.' Then he'd tell his colourful visitor what had happened so far in the show. Then they'd walk in, watch one number, and leave during the thunderous applause to move on to the theatre next door."

For a writer, this must have been a wonderful way to spend an evening, ducking from establishment to establishment, sampling the wares and measuring the competition. Not to mention for somebody not yet a decade into his full-time writing career, this was a magnificent opportunity to gain a hot-house education in the ways of Broadway, to glimpse what worked and what didn't, and to take the temperature of the most demanding theatre audience in the world. It was the sort of experience that surely could have been expected to inspire any writer to greater heights.

"Writing I regard as a way of life," said Behan in an interview with William Glover, drama critic of the Associated Press, at the end of October. "I know I'm happiest when I'm writing. My attitude to life is best expressed by Camus – the duty of a writer is not to those in power but to those who are subject to them. I think writers can do a lot to explain one man to another. I believe with Mencken that city people are better informed than country people. And I think the proper aim of all arts is the abolition of the village idiot."

Lofty thoughts from a writer at the peak of his powers and a man who'd gained a new perspective on the world from his vantage point in the heart of Manhattan.

"I wouldn't live in London under any circumstances, it doesn't even look like a city," said Behan. "But it does have the greatest theatre audience. I'd like to stay right here a good long time. But I don't have any wish to be a citizen. An Irish or a Norwegian passport is the best you can have these days. Any of the others and somebody hates you. If you have a Russian passport, half the world wants to get rid of you. And if you have an American passport, the other half hates you. Now I have no desire to see any other parts of America – miles and miles of prairies. The sight of so many subsidised farmers would make me physically ill."

The encounter with Glover was classic Behan at this time in his life, rambling on, delivering love letters one minute and firing poison arrows the next. "I was told it (New York) was hell so I must be a devil," he said about the city before then describing Staten Island, one of the outer boroughs and a place he visited to regularly to see his uncle, Jimmy Kearney, as "a hell-hole".

In what would be a recurring theme, he assured Glover he was working on "Richard's Cork Leg", a new play, and he would be returning to London in December to start on the pre-production planning for that. Three years later, he'd still be talking in exactly those terms about that work.

Still, he vowed to Glover he was on the dry and would be for some time. When they met, he told Glover they'd go to a saloon to conduct the interview but drank soda throughout and, not for the first time, professed a new abstemiousness. "I never wrote while drinking. It's all nonsense about liquor inspiring. I'm on water for the rest of my life, I hope. I feel I'm writing well. And if I drank, I wouldn't write at all."

Unfortunately, those words would prove sadly prophetic.

Drink Canada Dry

I went to the US Immigration and they gave me a pile of forms. I went to the Canadian place and they asked me if I had a union card. They warned me there wouldn't be much work as a house painter if I didn't have one, and was I coming over at my own expense. No, at yours, I said. I didn't fit any of the three categories but they gave me a visa anyway.

BRENDAN BEHAN, NOVEMBER 2, 1960

WHEN David Susskind started what was one of the first serious television talk shows on New York's Channel 13 in 1958, it was given the title "The Open End" for a very simple reason. Starting at 9pm on a Sunday night, the programme continued until he or his guests had had enough, even if that meant them debating for three or four hours. With that kind of remit, it was imperative to have serious talkers on the panel each week. On November 13th, 1960, the line-up for a show entitled "Backstage on Broadway" was typically impressive: Celeste Holm, Tennessee Williams, Anthony Quinn, Jack Lemmon, George Devine and Brendan Behan.

Even in that stellar company, Behan stood out, providing a couple of memorable moments. He sang "Lady Chatterley's Lover", announcing that it was a song from his forthcoming play "Richard's Cork Leg". He also delivered his share of quips, including the following verse about the birth of the Church of England:

Don't speak of your Protestant minister
Nor of his church without meaning or faith
For the foundation stone of his temple
Was the bollocks of Henry VIII

It wasn't an original composition but that didn't bother the millions chortling at home. Much like his drunken interlude with Malcolm Muggeridge on the BBC, the vulgarity did his public standing no harm at all.

Just under two weeks later, his services were in demand again for another high-profile event, this time off-camera. As he considered running for Mayor of New York City, Norman Mailer wanted to launch his campaign with a headline-grabbing party. Styling himself the representative of the dispossessed, he wished to host a shindig where he'd juxtapose homeless people and drug addicts with the most powerful and glamorous figures in town. His friend George Plimpton was handed a list of those he felt had to be present. Among the names were David Rockefeller, Prince Sadruddin (son of the Aga Khan) and Brendan Behan.

"Behan...represented Mailer's Dionysian side," wrote J. Michael Lennon in his biography of Mailer. "His radical IRA past and rumbustious escapades were enormously appealing to Mailer who later 'blessed' Behan for teaching him to perform in public."

On November 30th, Behan was the headline act at a meeting of the James Joyce Society at the Gotham Book Mart at West 47th Street. The lecture was formally titled "Brendan Behan on Joyce" but right from the introductory remarks, it was obvious he wasn't going to be delivering exactly that.

"Well, Ladies and Gentlemen," said Behan. "this colour is not my usual colour which is cholesterol red. I've never...I've never seen a really white person, only a dead one; but I have my normal Caucasian and ruddy hue. I understand I'm a Caucasian according to American statistics ...I'm a European by promotion; and I'm here tonight to talk to you about James Joyce. Well now, I suppose there are in this room half-a-dozen people who could tell you more, tell it to you technically better, about James Joyce, than I could."

That was by far the most accurate line of a rambling speech that touched only sporadically on the work of Joyce. Sounding very much like he was speaking without preparation and certainly evincing no great knowledge (nor did he claim any) about his fellow Dubliner, Behan went off on tangents that were entertaining enough, at least to those who presumably weren't put out by the complete lack of scholarship on offer. He namedropped profusely, admitted complete ignorance of "Finnegan's Wake", told a story about Joyce's sister Eileen asking him to write a book about James and his brother Stanislaus, and, mentioned how the forever-forthcoming "Richard's Cork Leg" owed its title to a story involving Joyce.

There were several telling details about the event. Aside from the bizarre fact that such an obviously improvised effort with no academic merit at all was later released as a vinyl record, there's also the matter of him using "effing" instead of "fucking" during one anecdote. As he pointed out himself, "The puritanism of the American television is, as you can see, catching..." He doesn't mention Beatrice being there but at one juncture he does point out the presence at the back of the room of Valerie Danby Smith who he told the crowd was "...Mr. Hemingway's secretary when she is not acting in a similar capacity for me." She would play a much larger role than that in his life down the road.

In the meantime, the Behans were headed north to Canada, a journey that ironically was going to take Brendan back to his past, to an autumn day in 1936 when members of the Irish Republican Army and various other interested parties came to St. Stephen's Green in the centre of Dublin for a peaceful demonstration. During the protest, Ambrose Victor Martin (later denounced in the Dail as a renowned communist) delivered a speech against the Fascists in the Spanish Civil War. At one point in the proceedings, a contingent representing the

Irish Christian Front (those in Ireland who sympathised with General Franco) appeared on the scene, carrying iron bars, bicycle chains, broken bottles, and an appetite for a fight with the IRA.

"As the IRA men prepared to defend themselves with their bare fists, a small boy with a wild shock of hair, ran from their ranks, waving a pistol nearly as big as himself and yelling a wonderful string of obscenities," wrote Eamonn Martin, son of Ambrose. "He stopped only a few feet from the Fronters and fired two shots close over their heads. They stopped in their tracks and the boy screamed, 'Get back you filth or I'll kill every bloody one of you!' The attackers didn't wait to count the bullets in his gun and I watched with delight as they retreated in hasty disorder. Brendan Behan, at thirteen, had saved my father and the others and set the pattern of impetuous behaviour that was to cause him so much trouble later on."

Young Martin and the gun-toting, adolescent Behan became friends and colleagues in Na Fianna, the youth wing of the movement. Later, Martin qualified as a barrister in Dublin and often represented Behan when he was involved in scrapes with the law. On one famous occasion, as the pair of them walked to the Four Courts, Behan asked his buddy and legal brief to jump into the Liffey so he could save him, arrive before the judge dripping wet and be let off the charge of assaulting a garda because of his heroics. Martin refused to jump.

By 1960 Martin was living in Toronto, Canada. Being 500 miles from New York meant he received constant invitations from his old pal to come down and visit, Behan phoned regularly and beseeched Martin to let his son Maoliosa visit New York so he could show the lad the sights. He had always been fond of the child. When he found himself en route to Dundrum Court on the day of Maoliosa's third birthday, he stopped off at the Martins' to give the boy a present. Now, the self-styled, uncrowned king of New York, he was thrilled when Martin came to visit so he could give his son the gift of the city.

Aside from visiting all the usual landmarks, he also afforded Maoliosa a unique opportunity not offered on any normal tourist itinerary. One evening, the pair of them stood in the wings at the Cort Theatre, watching a performance of "The Hostage". When Behan gave the signal, the duo then hared across the stage, much to the bemusement of the actors and the audience.

"The trip ended poorly for Mel (Maoliosa)," wrote Martin. "He posed with Brendan while smoking a huge Havana cigar, unaware that a photographer was capturing his devilment for the rest of the world – including his school principal and me – to see. He came home to a hot reception, even if he had smoked his first cigar with the great Brendan Behan."

When Behan booked a pair of speaking engagements in Montreal in the first week of December, his old friend from Dublin was charged with the job of driving him to the Quebecois city. The trip was the brainchild of Tony Aspler. As a student at Trinity College, Aspler had crossed paths with Behan and, deciding that a dose of his wit and wisdom was badly needed in Canada, he'd persuaded McGill University and the Comedie Canadienne to host and finance the gigs. Interestingly, the local media and the city's Irish club showed no great appetite for Behan's visit, one feeling he wasn't box office enough, the other worried about how his antics might reflect negatively upon his compatriots in Montreal.

Behan arrived in Canada, two days before his first lecture. Unfortunately, this coincided with a cold snap that sent temperatures plummeting to 15 degrees below and blanketed the city with snow. This inhibited his natural tendency to move around and sample the delights of a new town, especially one that delighted in the nickname "La Belle Ville".

"If he could not saunter around a new city, talking to

doormen, paper boys, buying magazines, he was unhappy," recalled Aspler. "Now, caged in his hotel room, the prospects for the week were dismal indeed...So we toured the city – and we only got out of the car at the look-out on the top of Mount Royal to see the snowscape of Montreal sliding gently down into the grey St. Lawrence like a ski slope. Brendan made the sign of the cross over the sullen city and then urinated in the snow."

The last act summed up his approach to the next few days. He fell spectacularly from the wagon and appeared determined to piss off as many people as he could in the time available. That first night, at Behan's insistence, they visited the city's French Quarter where during a meal he disappeared briefly before returning and starting into a cocktail of champagne and Guinness. Soon fortified by the Black Velvets, he was regaling the other customers with a lusty rendition of "Lady Chatterley's Lover", now the go-to song in his repertoire. Halfway through this bawdy number, he decided it was time to embark on a pub crawl through a part of the city known as The Main.

Predictably, Behan found the vibe and the company in an area notorious for rough bars, prostitution, doss houses and 15 cent movie theatres, much to his liking. Indeed, he shocked journalists who later asked him for his thoughts about Montreal by eulogising The Main, describing the characters he met there as "fine citizens" and denouncing those who believed otherwise as "bigots and snobs".

What else did they expect him to say? His trip through the Tenderloin (another name for it) was vintage Behan on the binge as he wended his way from bar to bar. The sight of the French language signs inspired him to start singing "La Marseillaise". Eyewitnesses testified he gave some or all of the French national anthem in every establishment he visited. The sight of the drunken Irishman, his hair all over his face, his shirt opened to the waist, was enough to draw a crowd and, indeed, to spawn an entourage. If they came for the spectacle, they stayed because his generosity and his celebrity kept the drink flowing freely.

"Do you know the Marseillaise," Behan asked the musicians on the stage of one nightclub on Amherst Street. "Well, play it and I'll sing it."

In this place, the anthem was only the opening number. He went on to deliver several more from his extensive back catalogue of Irish ballads and folk songs. Aspler remembered him singing, "hands clasped in front of him, eyes closed, swaying slightly" and then making a very bizarre request. He wanted to visit Aspler's parents. No problem. It was well after midnight when Behan and his now-enlarged entourage rolled in the door of a small, two-bedroom apartment on Queen Mary Road where Mrs. Aspler immediately began cooking for her famous guest.

Under the peculiar circumstances, everything was going reasonably well until the power went out. Then convinced he'd been struck by blindness, the drunk Behan tripped over a coffee table and hit the floor. Sprawled out on the carpet, unconscious, they put a blanket over him and he went off to sleep. Next morning, Tony Aspler woke up to the sound of banging cupboard doors in the kitchen and the sight of a naked playwright desperately searching for something, anything that might serve as the hair of the dog.

Within hours of the party ending, showing the serial drinker's capacity for refueling, he was at the breakfast table, devouring a plate of steak tartare, accompanied by a raw egg, served to him by the bemused Mrs. Aspler. Soon, he was ready to go again.

He was booked into the Royal Embassy Hotel where, once word of his antics got around, previously disinterested journalists from newspapers and radio came in search of some easy copy. Of course, he gave it to him. When a journalist mentioned that the swanky hotel had formally opened when Liberace stayed there in 1956, he quipped: "Yeah? And four years later, Behan came and closed it." He didn't quite close it but he certainly gave them a visit they wouldn't forget in a hurry.

"He's on a monumental binge," said one of the hotel staff. "I've never seen anything like it in this hotel."

When management intervened and tried to get him to tone down the cabaret, he reacted in his usual uncooperative style. He ramped up the volume of his singing and exaggerated the play-acting. He began marching up and down the lobby singing, "I'm the king of the castle, get down you dirty rascal" while swigging from a bottle. Reporters gleefully taking note of his antics for the next day's papers couldn't figure out what he was saying half the time, between the slurring of the words and the frequent lapsing into Irish. They did, however, manage to get the gist of some of the insults.

What did he think of Montreal?

"It could be worse, it could be Toronto!"

There was more damning with faint praise.

"If I was an Englishman here, I'd become French! Canada is mitigated by the French.'

Whether it was Beatrice's intervention or his own realisation that he had a public event to prepare for, he was back on the dry by dinner time on the night before he was due to give his first lecture. Indeed, he put on a dinner jacket and braces, no small deal for a man the looseness of whose pants were becoming the stuff of intercontinental legend. Of course, even sober, he couldn't resist joining the band in the restaurant for a couple of songs. Drunk or dry, the stage always beckoned and the performer always had to perform.

During this particular cameo, the trip took another unexpected turn. On returning to his table, Behan was assailed by a woman with a Northern Irish accent.

"I'm from Belfast," she said.

"I won't hold that against you," said Behan.

From there, they hit it off and Behan and his company were invited back to the woman's home on the other side of the island of Montreal. The offer was politely declined and the evening ended without incident. The calm before the storm.

"The following day was the Feast of the Immaculate Conception which meant that every bar in the province was closed," wrote Aspler. "At 8.30 am, I had a frantic phone call from Beatrice to say that he had disappeared. After trying all his haunts, I remembered the woman from Belfast. I phoned her and in the background, I could hear music and Brendan's voice roaring above it, 'Glory-o, Glory-o to the bold Fenian men....' Beatrice, Eamonn (Martin) and I drove out to collect him."

Inevitably, extracting the target from the location wasn't quite a surgical operation. When the raiding party arrived at the house, they discovered Behan in the middle of a traditional music and drinking session. There were drums, a fiddle, an accordion and a drunken playwright leading the impromptu band. Just as his wife and minders entered the room, Behan took umbrage at one of his fellow performers and a fight broke out. The incident culminated in his wife and minders dragging him to the car and to safety as his new friends turned quickly into his worst enemies.

It was early enough in the day for Aspler to believe that a major disaster had been averted. With the bars closed, there seemed every chance of drying Behan out and delivering him sober to his speaking engagement that evening. That hope died at lunch when a starstruck restauranteur gave the quartet four complimentary Irish coffees. Behan downed three of them, started into the wine and, suddenly, his appointment at the college seemed in grave danger.

A spectacularly beautiful campus at the foot of Mount Royal in downtown Montreal, McGill University was named for a Scottish immigrant whose money funded the establishment of the institution in 1821. Since then, it had become one of the best schools in the country, often described as Canada's equivalent to America's vaunted Ivy League. Behan's fee for his lecture was $500 and students were being charged $1 and $2 for tickets to the event. Aspler was so concerned about Behan's deteriorating condition that he began downing his drinks when he wasn't looking. A brave move and to very little avail. Eventually, he knew what he had to do and in late afternoon, the promoter phoned the university to try get the gig postponed.

This led to an announcement on local radio telling people that the lecture had been cancelled but 450 students and faculty still turned up. Most of them had heard rumours of Behan's antics, many perhaps came because they feared missing out on some memorable havoc. In any case, they sat for an hour and waited in case he came.

"This is awful," said one university official. "What could have got into him?"

"Liquor!" roared a student from the front row.

Eventually, somebody made an executive decision to clear the hall. "The event is cancelled and your money will be refunded," said the official on the stage. With that, the crowd dispersed to the hallway outside where they gathered around tables to get back the price of their admission. That was the chaotic scene that Behan came upon and boldly strode through. His hair all over the place, his shirt opened one button too many and wearing the stains of a day's drinking, this dissolute figure threw his overcoat on the stage, posed for a lone photographer and then made for the microphone. Much to the delight of those who'd come on the off-chance of mischief and merrymaking.

"I understand I'm not being paid for this performance I don't want your fee. I'll talk for nothing. See, you've succeeded in doing what Jack Paar could not do. You've got me here for nothing. I had intended to come here and insult you as hard as I know how and I intended to tell you about Samuel Butler!"

During a visit almost a century earlier, Butler, a famous poet of the time, summed up the dreariness of the town with the refrain: "Oh God, oh Montreal".

Regardless of the fee, he made good on his promise to insult as he delivered in his own inimitable slurred fashion his verdict on French policies in North Africa and demanded French-speaking Canadians do more to stop this.

"I don't like Nazis – I don't like French Nazis any more than I like German Nazis. I like France. They entertained me last year but now they are murdering Algerians. Montrealers love France but now France is led by madmen, gangsters and collaborators. If you won't stop them who will? What can those other idiots – I can't call them Canadians, because they're not and I can't call them Indians – what can they do to help Algeria?"

There were enough controversial opinions to thrill and appall the audience and to generate plenty of headlines the next morning.

"This place reminds me of a Victorian living room," said Behan as he finished up. "I've enjoyed talking to you here."

With that, he came down off the stage and was engulfed by students besotted by the demented character in their midst. Soon, he headed out into the night, a pie-eyed Piper with a group of undergraduates that one press report put at around 100 for company.

Joseph Napoleon Servant was the night steward at the Montreal Men's Press Club at the Laurentinian Hotel on Dorchester Street. It was there that Behan and his shoal of followers washed up. Surprisingly, everything went fine for a while as the master entertained the students. Eventually, however, Servant decided the visiting author's language was just too profane for the club. He asked him to tone it down and when he didn't comply, he and his party were ejected. Not without the obligatory fight of course.

"Behan came charging at my right fist when a woman – I think it was his wife – got him in a headlock," said Servant. "And she dragged him through the door, one minute there was a hundred people in the club the next there were three."

The sober Behan of the early days in New York was now a distant memory.

"His liver's like an old hobnail boot," said one anonymous 'friend' to the Montreal Gazette as he continued to rampage through the city the next day.

He ended up sick in his hotel bed. Not drink-sick, actually sick. A doctor came and gave him a B-12 shot but mostly he just lay there for days. For a man who'd been off the drink for so much of the previous year, the damage being done to his diabetic body was enormous and taking a very obvious toll. Aspler cancelled the Comedie Canadienne appearance and Behan, when he finally recovered some semblance of his normal self, decried his new surroundings.

"I'm fuckin' lousy. I'm fuckin' lousy. I'm fuckin' drunk and I'm not even fuckin' happy. I wish to fuck I hadn't left New York," said Behan during a phone call to Leonard Lyons back in New York. "Why don't you come rescue me? I'm hell-holed in this place. I wish I had never come here. New York's the only place on this continent where you have an excuse for being."

More than three months after leaving Dublin for New York, it was time to go home. His antics as much as his celebrity ensured even his departure from Canada was assiduously tracked by journalists.

"I hate to leave this city but I've got to get back to Ireland," Behan lied to reporters, sipping soda water in the club car of the train at Windsor Station, on the way to Halifax to catch a liner. "She's a fascinating city. She's half New Orleans, which has kept up a phony French atmosphere and half-American. What I mean is that your city has all the good points of New Orleans and America. Montreal has given me a cold and that's why I couldn't give my other talk like I was supposed to."

Obviously, he'd learned from previous mistakes, giving the press what they wanted to hear about their town rather than what he really thought.

"I watched Brendan standing at the window, the last time I was to see him: ashen-faced, dishevelled, his collar turned up against the biting wind," wrote Aspler. "The man was going home, leaving his myth behind him. In seven days his name was a household word in Montreal: idolised by the students, badgered by the press, lionised and fawned over, criticised and neglected, Brendan Behan had left a mark on the city. Glory-o, Glory-o to the bold Fenian man."

He had left a mark on Aspler too. He would turn his crazy week in the company of Behan into the material for his first novel "The Streets of Askelon". In it, the hero Bart O'Shea, an alcoholic poet and a very blatant facsimile of Behan, gets involved in various misadventures and wages a kind of war on the city of Montreal.

"Alcohol is the enemy of the writer," said Behan, doing one last interview on the leg of the train journey from Truro to Halifax. "I am not against alcohol. People wouldn't be interested in my vital statistics – pints, quarts, nips, that is. But I am inclined to drink a little more than I should."

The carousing and partying of the previous week ensured his arrival in Halifax was something of an event. As he and Beatrice disembarked from the train, a crowd of about 25 gathered around him, and he was still playing to the gallery even as the Cunard liner Saxonia, the ship that was to take them home to Ireland, was waiting at the docks. On December 20th 1960, the Saxonia arrived back in Cobh where a cameraman was on hand to capture Behan walking off the ship with a suitcase in his hand and a legend that now stretched all the way across the Atlantic Ocean.

CHAPTER EIGHT

The St. Patrick's Day Massacre

The more successful you become the more of a target you are for every bum with a glass of whiskey in his hand. Gene Tunney told me he had the same problem because every American wanted a poke at him. It's becoming that way with me now. The more famous I become the more enemies I seem to have

BRENDAN BEHAN, SCHENECTADY GAZETTE, FEBRUARY 10, 1961

HAVING moved theatres twice, "The Hostage" was due to end its run on Broadway with its 127th performance on January 7th, 1961. That morning, Brendan Behan accompanied his friend Jim Downey to Dublin airport. After a visit to Ireland, the restauranteur was heading back to New York.

"Jim you'll be there tonight," said Behan. "I want you to go to the closing and get the cast around you and read them this note."

On a scrap of paper in the bar, he got to work.

Dear Pippins of the Big Apple,
Any playwright, actor, scene-shifter, director or doorman who is not on Broadway is in exile. I love your bright lights and your bright faces. My pilgrimage to your holy land has been, for me, a spiritual awakening. It also did my liver a bit of good. May God bless Broadway as Broadway blesses the world. My love until we meet again.
Brendan Behan

During that final performance, Caroline Burke Swann took liberty with the text and inserted herself into the action. She put a chair onstage, and, in full view of the audience, she sat there, drinking milk for the duration, a rather avant-garde or post-modern moment. Why did the co-producer of the play do this? "I felt I owed it to Brendan." He might have been 3000 miles from Broadway but America wasn't going to forget him in a hurry.

On January 20th, 1961, John F. Kennedy was sworn in as the 35th President of the United States of America. The historic nature of the event and the magnetic attraction of the newly-elected leader drew gaggles of celebrities to a snow-blasted Washington DC. The pre-inauguration night bash was put together by Frank Sinatra, Hollywood was liberally represented by the likes of Bette Davis, Laurence Olivier and Milton Berle, and Kennedy's speech at the Capitol was post-scripted by Robert Frost reading his poem "The Gift Outright".

Weeks earlier, an official invitation had been sent out by The White House, bearing the rather basic address: Mr. and Mrs. Brendan Behan, Dublin, Ireland. While the letter reached the Behans at 5 Anglesea Road in Ballsbridge, the house Brendan had bought with the proceeds from "Borstal Boy", in plenty of time for them to travel, they thought better of it.

If the playwright remained out of sight of America, some there still had him very much at the front of their minds.

Alexander H. Cohen grew up in a duplex penthouse on Park Avenue where some of his fondest childhood memories revolved, not around a rather distant mother and a cold stepfather, but a pair of warm Irish spinsters named Catherine and Mary who cared for him and his brother Gerry. At just 21 years old, Cohen used an inheritance to start dabbling in producing theatre, enjoying spectacular successes (he introduced Marcel Marceau to American audiences) and failures (critics dubbed him the millionaire boy angel) in equal measure. Along the way, he also gained a reputation for high living (he would eventually own houses in London, France, and the Virgin Islands).

By early 1961, Cohen was entering his third decade in show business. Having just completed the supervising of the construction of the O'Keefe Centre, a 3100 seat theatre in Toronto, commissioned by the brewing family of the same name, he remained tasked with booking and managing the new venue for the first year of its existence.

Evincing his usual keen eye for new talent and for avant-garde risk-taking, he put together a show he called "Impulse", an ambitious jazz revue to be headlined by Art Blakey and the Jazz Messengers, also featuring African percussionist Babatunde Olatunji, and a rising chanteuse called Nina Simone.

"America's one indisputable contribution to the art world is jazz," said Cohen when launching the venture, "and it's high time it found its way to the Broadway Stage."

Cohen's plan was for "Impulse" to spend an initial week at the O'Keefe Centre from March 20th, knocking the edges off the production before transferring down to New York for a March 29th open on Broadway. With over 40 musicians involved in the various acts, he had only one man in mind for the difficult job of compering such an action-packed evening's entertainment – Brendan Behan.

"An MC merely introduces acts, 'Impulse' will have a theme and Mr. Behan will have a point of view," Cohen told reporters early in February. When the journalists asked him what qualified Behan for this particular role, Cohen replied simply: "He digs it."

Beatrice Behan didn't dig it when the offer from Cohen arrived at their home. The first few weeks of 1961 had already been typically tumultuous even by Behan standards. Brendan was back drinking heavily, his appetite inevitably heightened by a series of professional setbacks. His producer Joan Littlewood had been unimpressed by his work-in-progress

"Richard's Cork Leg" when he read extracts of it to her, and Gael-Linn had asked him to rewrite a one-act play in Irish called "A Fine Day in the Graveyard".

The latter request – which he interpreted as an outright rejection rather than constructive criticism – prompted an ugly incident in Smyths of the Green, one of Dublin's tonier establishments. In the usual Behan way, a simple excursion to purchase bottles of champagne to drown his sorrows culminated in a headline-generating fracas, more fighting when the Gardai came to the shop, and a soap operatic day in the District Court when he was lucky to escape with a fine of £30 and a reprimand from Justice O'Hagan.

This then was the troubled character Alexander Cohen felt was just the man to anchor his eclectic new show that was destined to wow New York, just the persona to deliver witty bon mots to the audience as the musicians rushed on and off the stage between sets.

"You'll only be bored in a jazz review," said Beatrice when the offer came, replete with a $500 advance to show Cohen meant business.

"What do you mean?" asked Brendan.

"I mean, 'You're not a jazzman Brendan', you'll just go on another bash. Write to Cohen and tell him you can't go."

In her autobiography, Beatrice later admitted she hoped by this point her husband had left America behind him. And if he wasn't moved to travel by Kennedy's invitation to the inauguration, she was perfectly entitled to think that. She also knew him well enough to realise returning to New York, whatever the reason or motivation, wasn't going to do anything but exacerbate his drinking. At least in Dublin, she always felt she knew roughly (most of the time) who he was with and where he was. Manhattan was, as she'd already discovered during their troubled stay the previous year, a very different prospect in that regard. Initially, Brendan appeared to listen to her counsel and he rebuffed Cohen's offer.

"After a great deal of discussion and consideration, I have decided I cannot appear on your show, 'Impulse', this March," he wrote in a letter to the impresario. "Owing to commitments to my publishers, both in American and England, as well as pressure from my London producer who expects my new play to open at the end of March, I find myself in this position. I am sorry for any inconvenience which may arise out of this, and I hope at some future date to avail of your offer in New York."

Beatrice's relief at keeping him home was to be short-lived. Befitting somebody so suited to the role of Broadway Svengali that Woody Allen later cast him as one in "The Purple Rose of Cairo", Cohen remained dogged in his pursuit of his man. He cabled a six-page missive to Ballsbridge, imploring Brendan to sign on. Beatrice claimed Cohen played up how much money he'd invested and would lose without Behan's presence. Perhaps he did. It's doubtful though that this was much of a genuine consideration given that Cohen was a man who wagered, won and lost hundreds of thousands on productions every year of his career. Whatever he did manage to do, whatever persuasive power he invoked, the impresario succeeded in changing Behan's mind. New York beckoned once more.

As the Cunard liner Queen Elizabeth sailed to New York in early March with the Behans on board, the new edition of "Who's Who" was published in London and Brendan was an entry for the first time, his recreations listed as "drinking, writing and swimming." A reporter from the Daily Mail phoned the ship to ask him about this latest accolade and his interest in swimming. "Yes I'm a swimmer," said Behan, "it's a great cure for hangovers."

On March 13th, a beaming Brendan and a somewhat less enthusiastic Beatrice arrived in New York. As the Queen

Elizabeth docked at Pier 90 near West 50th Street on the North River, a photographer from the Daily News captured him, calmly sipping tea and smoking a cigar. "I'm off the drink for Lent," he told reporters, "and for breadth too!"

That the paparazzo felt him worthy of this attention at all speaks volumes about the type of celebrity he had become during his previous sojourn. If the shot is very much a portrait of the artist in repose, it was to be at odds with so much of what happened to him for the rest of his stay. Ever before he hooked up with Cohen and the jazz musicians, there was controversy. Plenty of it.

Once they heard he was coming back to town, the Gaelic Society of Fordham University had invited him to march with them in the St. Patrick's Day parade in Manhattan that Friday. Just like tens of thousands of Irish and Irish-Americans were due to do. Except, there was one slight problem. Behan was regarded as radioactive by the organisers of the event. They'd seen the havoc he'd wreaked across the city over the previous autumn, endured the constant negative headlines, and witnessed the ribald television appearances. Ignoring the fact the parade itself is one large alcohol-fuelled affair anyway, they moved quickly to ban him from marching. The Gaelic Society of Fordham, who'd previously run foul of parade authorities for trying to march a live ram in their contingent, was disinvited too.

"We have a semi-religious, almost sacred feeling about this parade," said James J. Comerford, a Justice of the Court of Special Sessions, a member of the parade organising committee, and a Fordham alumnus. "We don't want a personality who has been advertised so extensively as a common drunk."

Those who knew him would have expected nothing less from Comerford. A judge who used to denounce critics of his draconian sentencing as "liberal liberals", New York magazine once described him as "a stern and sour arbiter of morals, given to tough sentences (30 years and 30 Hail Marys!) – a no-nonsense man whose vision of right and wrong is as clear as Waterford glass."

While Harry M. Hynes was the chairman of the parade committee, Comerford was regarded as the most influential figure on the board and the man responsible for banning Behan. The irony is the two of them had a lot in common. Both had enjoyed paramilitary careers with the Irish Republican Army as young men before going on to achieve renown without weapons in their hands. Born on the family farm in Coolraheen, County Kilkenny in 1901, Comerford joined the F Company Third Battalion of the Kilkenny Brigade of the IRA at the age of 16, reaching the rank of captain before his 21st birthday.

Shot by the Black and Tans during the War of Independence, he ended up moving to New York where he went to university by night before embarking on a successful legal career. The former teenage rebel somehow became synonymous with the stern and rigorous dispatch of justice from the bench in his adopted city. If there was a complete opposite to the caricature of the bawdy, drunken, gregarious Irishman that Behan styled himself then, the stern and taciturn Comerford was it.

"We heard through the grapevine that all Behan wanted to do was get in the parade and then break out of it at the reviewing stand to shake hands with Cardinal Spellman," said Comerford. "He thought this was a way to get his book sanctified."

Well, if Behan did want publicity for his book (which hardly needed it given the American edition of "Borstal Boy" sold 20,000 copies in just one month), he got plenty of it via the decision to stop him from marching. During the one time of year when all things Irish are in vogue in the American media, the

New York papers suddenly had a good old-fashioned ruckus, some ethnic infighting punctuated by colourful intervals of public name-calling.

"By Jaysus," said Behan of the parade organisers, "they'd put years on you with their plastic shamrocks and their green socks."

Willy Brandt, the Mayor of West Berlin, was the esteemed guest of honour for the parade but his presence was reduced to the status of a sideshow by the Behan row.

"While the parade committee was beckoning Herr Brandt with one hand," wrote the New York Times, "it was barring Brendan Behan the Irish playwright with the other."

Once news broke of his expulsion, the invitations started to come in from parade organisers in other cities. Boston was quick off the mark, so too Holyoke, a town in Western Massachusetts initially settled by emigrants from Dingle and once known as Ireland Parish. London, Ontario made an attempt to bring him north of the border. In the end, he opted for somewhere closer to his temporary home.

"We're not running a high-brow silk stocking Irish event," said Edward Casey, chairman of the Jersey City St. Patrick's Day festivities when Behan accepted their offer to receive the key to the city on March 17th. "We have a quart of milk ready for him. If he doesn't want to drink it straight, he can use it in his tea."

Of course, Behan wasn't done with the crowd in New York yet. He threatened to march anyway, regardless of the ban, joking that he'd opt out before the reviewing stand in case Comerford spotted him and gave him "six months". It says much for his standing in the country that Newsweek magazine offered him a platform to write about the controversy. He didn't hold back with his retaliation. The polemic included an attack on Irish-Americans for their attitude to March 17th...

"...I suppose there are some prudish people in America, just like everywhere. They want to look like Queen Victoria's husband. If someone drank a glass of Irish whiskey or stout, it would do a lot of good for the old country, rather than hanging shamrocks around your ears..."

And a wonderful takedown of their outdated view of the home country.

"...We don't have leprechauns, paddys in top hats, and magic mists. We're proud of our hydroelectric plants, our transport, and our housing, none of which are run by leprechauns. We are now wiping out tuberculosis, and we're prouder of all that than all the blather about Glocca Maura."

Then, there was his trademark gag laced with bitterness.....

"...I now have a new theory on what happened to the snakes when St Patrick drove them out of Ireland. They came to New York and became judges..."

And the inevitable show of erudition...

"...I recommend the judge to read the Confessions of St Patrick, in which he said, 'the honest man must walk as warily as a deer, not so much for fear of the enemies of Christianity as for fear of those who pretend to be better Christians than the Apostles.' I do not set myself up as an Apostle but I think that I can afford to be more open with my sinfulness than Judge Comerford..."

And the odd sideswipe at non-Dubliners.

"...I think they (fire engines) must all be driven by Micks from the mountains who were fed up with all the silence and like to make a lot of noise."

The press loved the whole brouhaha. Well, most of them did. In a sign that perhaps the city, or at least some of its most prominent residents, were tiring of the Behan show, the New York Daily News took the side of the parade organisers in an editorial on March 16th.

"For our part, we're glad Justice Comerford thumbed Behan to the sidelines," went the piece. "Tomorrow's parade should be much the better for the absence of a show-off whose antics, frankly, are threatening to become as boring as Lady Loverley's chatter or any six imitators of Edgar Bergen, Charlie McCarthy and Mortimer Snerd. Jersey City can have him."

This just added fuel to the fire. Behan wrote back to the paper immediately. In a wide-ranging letter published on St. Patrick's Day, he denounced leader-writers, describing them all as university graduates lacking the talent to become professional creative writers or the application to become proper writers. While he felt their "little essays" usually interested nobody, he could not let this particular attack go without retaliating.

"Your leader writer says he is bored by my off-and-on the bottle antics," wrote Behan. "He is not more bored than I, by newspaper reports of my personal activities, habits and failings. Through no fault of mine, the newspapers began reporting these things. They can stop reporting them whenever they wish and stick to more serious matters such as unemployment. The cure is in the hands of The News and every other newspaper that thinks my drinking habits (or non-drinking habits) are of interest to the ordinary readers. They can leave my tea or champagne statistics out of the news columns, where they don't belong anyway. See you in Jersey City."

An estimated 125,000 marched up Fifth Avenue on St. Patrick's Day. The sky overhead was pristine blue but a cold breeze whipped along the city streets, ensuring the parade moved at pace before reaching the reviewing party of Mayor Brandt, Cardinal Spellman and New York's own Mayor Robert F. Wagner. The crowds gathered to watch could often be seen marching on the spot trying to keep warm. Behan was not among them. He was on his way to Jersey, travelling in a Cadillac that he felt "befits my station". Of his journey across the river, he later remarked rather grandiloquently: "At one end of the Holland Tunnel (that links Jersey and Manhattan) lies freedom. I choose it."

On the steps of Jersey City Hall, a large group had gathered, mostly men in suits and fedoras, some holding up "Welcome Behan" signs like groupies at an election rally. The votes on this ballot were already in and Behan posed somewhat sheepishly for photographers as he collected his prize, the key to the city, from Mayor Charles Witkowski. Beatrice stood between them, a fur stole draped over her shoulders, her handbag in front of her, as the cameras flashed.

"This has moved me more than I can say. This is the best St. Patrick's Day ever for me," said Behan to the band of reporters who'd been dispatched across the river to cover his appearance, perhaps by editors hoping or expecting him to do something controversial. "Maybe I should send a note of thanks to those in New York for not letting me wear myself out marching so I could be over here enjoying myself. The people of New Jersey made up for it. New Jersey is the Latin Quarter of New York. New York is the duller part."

In some of the photographs taken that day, Behan, conforming to the Irish-American diktat by wearing a garish green tie under his suit, is also captured waving a 100-year old Blackthorn shillelagh stick in the air that he subsequently gifted to the mayor. Indeed, at one juncture, he posed near the Jersey docks, pointing across the river, cocking a snoot at New York in the background. Following the key-giving ceremony, the party moved on for luncheon at Casino-in-the-Park where Behan gave his audience the type of performance they expected. After the food, the singing started and despite drinking nothing stronger than Club Soda, he delivered several of his party-pieces, including "Molly Malone", much to the delight of all present.

"His cousin, Paul Bourke, who lived in New Jersey, drove us across for the ceremony and Brendan entered into the celebrations as though he were at the White House," wrote Beatrice. "He could count Irish-Americans among his friends, but I knew by now that the attitude of some of them annoyed him."

That night, he made it back to New York in good time. He had to. He had a prior engagement at "The Blue Angel", a club on East 55th Street. For 18 years, this place had been one of the more glamorous and eclectic venues in the city. Behan had got to know Max Gordon, one of the co-owners and an individual who'd built his reputation blooding future headline acts like Barbra Streisand, Mort Sahl, Dick Gregory, Eartha Kitt, Bobby Short, and the fabled comic duo of Elaine May and Mike Nichols (later to gain fame directing movies). As soon as it emerged he was coming back to the city, Gordon had booked Behan to play the Blue Angel on St. Patrick's night, billing him as "a cabaret act". A description very few people who knew him would have argued with.

Having stayed on the straight and narrow in Jersey, he made it to the gig in good shape, strolling up to the door, accompanied by Shelley Berman, a Blue Angel stalwart and one of the most talked-about of a new generation of edgy stand-up comics around town. Once he saw Behan, the bouncer's face lit up. He was Irish too.

"Are there many of our own inside?" asked Brendan of his compatriot.

"I hate that expression, 'our own', Brendan," said Berman, before the bouncer could even answer the question. "Everyone is your own."

On another night, that sort of contrary comment might have been a red rag to a bull. But sober and in the company of a comic whose work he respected and whose advice and counsel he may have needed before going on stage, Behan saw wisdom in his new friend's comment. Especially when Berman followed up with an explanation of how his father had been mistreated by one of his "own" upon arriving in America from Russia at the turn of the century.

"We went into the Blue Angel and although I'm not a professional in the gagging game, one section of my family has been in the theatre business and in show business generally, supplying costumes, running theatres, owning cinemas and all to that effect for generations," wrote Behan. "Anyway, I got up and did my piece and I succeeded in making Shelley Berman laugh, and as he is a professional in the business, I consider him a fair critic. I can put on a show for an hour perhaps once in every two weeks, but I couldn't do as well as these professional guys every night. However, that night Berman laughed, and I don't think he was just being polite. Well maybe he was. Afterwards we all sang Irish songs, some of which I made up myself."

A St Patrick's day which began in controversy and carried the potential for disaster had turned into a very positive affair. The successful trip to Jersey City had been followed by a well-received stand-up/monologue cameo at a prestigious venue in midtown. When he heard how well Behan had gone down in the cabaret, how professionally he'd comported himself, Alexander Cohen must have been very pleased at having the foresight to hire him to MC his jazz show. Unfortunately, that good feeling wasn't going to last too long. There were headlines coming. Plenty of them.

CHAPTER NINE

Chief Firewater And All That Jazz

Brendan's drinking has nothing to do with publicity. Like millions of other people he drinks to relax. He happens to be the type who can't drink in moderation

BEATRICE BEHAN, TORONTO, MARCH 19TH, 1961

IN 1955, Nathan Phillips became Mayor of Toronto after a ground-breaking election. The first Jew to hold the office, his appointment marked a significant break with tradition and a seismic shift in municipal politics. To that point in its history, every mayor of the city had been Protestant and the position had been monopolised by members of the city's powerful Orange Order throughout the first half of the 20th century. Indeed, the Orangeman that Phillips unseated had run into trouble for controversial comments about the Battle of the Boyne and for running his re-election campaign with the rather restrictive slogan, "Leslie Saunders – Protestant".

This then was the place to which Brendan Behan took the train from New York on March 19th, 1961. Befitting the city's supposedly new, more ecumenical atmosphere, one of his first stops was at City Hall where he was met by Phillips, living up to his reputation as "mayor of all the people". If Behan had done his homework, immediately reminding Phillips that the town went by the nickname "Toronto the Good", a legacy of its days as a bastion of Victorian morality back in the 19th century, Phillips knew something of the character of his visitor too.

"If you have any trouble with this fellow while you're in Toronto, you just report to me," the mayor said to Beatrice while wagging his finger jokingly at the smiling Behan. All was good and jovial during a pleasant half an hour in Phillips' office in an imposing building on the corner of Queen and Bay Streets.

"Truth to tell, Mr. Behan was on his best behaviour at a meeting in his honor's office, and the mayor was just kidding," went a report in the Quebec Chronicle-Telegraph. "Behan didn't destroy any furniture, didn't use even a teeny weeny bad word, and just swapped badinage for half an hour."

That the press were present for the encounter said much about the needs of the two men. Behan was trying to drum up publicity for Alexander Cohen's jazz revue, and Phillips, aside from realising he was in the company of one of the biggest celebrities of the moment, must have known rolling out the red carpet for a Dubliner with an IRA pedigree would seriously irk his Orange opponents. Certainly, the tone of the newspaper coverage of Behan's visit had an abrasive edge to it. Witness this quote from the Toronto Globe and Mail under the headline "Notes by Sage of Nonsense".

"Brendan Behan was not drinking yesterday when he arrived in Toronto," wrote Arthur Brydon. "He was talking, cursing, guffawing, snorting and spouting sparks and ashes all over the rugs of the Royal York Hotel. Waving a cigar which kept frustrating him by going out, he added a new target to his long list of hates, the invasion of London's Fleet Street by Canadian proprietors...Mr. Behan's condition vis-à-vis the consumption of alcohol was somewhat in doubt but it was reported that considerable drinking had been going on. A man who had been his companion since Mr. Behan arrived by train in the early morning hours reinforced this report by leaning forward to light a cigarette and falling on his face."

Brydon captured the mood perfectly. Behan had spent the journey north drinking and, Beatrice noted, the more he consumed the worse his form seemed to get. She had a bad feeling about the city the moment they stepped from the train, her concerns only exacerbated after they checked into their room on the seventh floor of the York Hotel.

"We received abusive telephone calls telling us that Brendan wasn't welcome and that he should take himself back to Ireland," she wrote. "We knew, of course, that there was a strong Orange feeling in the city and that an Irish Republican like Brendan, despite his reputation as a dramatist, wasn't welcome."

For all the foreboding and the historical nastiness, Behan had delivered the goods for the journalists who crowded around him at the hotel, in search of copy. There was the usual scattergun of Behanisms, covering all sorts of ground.

From the venue for the show....

"Your O'Keefe Centre looks to me like a sanctified garage. Yet it's a wonderfully big theatre and the acoustics are good."

To his knowledge of music...

"I can't read a note of music but I can certainly read a cheque."

To bravado about drink...

"On the wagon is an amateur phrase. You'd never hear it from a professional alcoholic. It's a tribute to the sheltered life of the person who uses the expression."

To the local customs...

"Your Toronto liquor laws (a lot more restrictive than in the US) are good enough for you because you're used to them. For me, they're a puzzlement..."

To his impressions of Toronto and its citizens...

"I like Toronto, it's not Dublin of course. The difference is that there's not the scurrilous talk here that there is in Dublin. I dread to think what they're saying about me in Dublin now that I'm not there. It's not that the Irish are cynical. It's rather that they have a wonderful lack of respect for everything and everybody. A Torontonian is a fellow who leaves the arts to his wife. He does this because he thinks it's a sort of feminine for a real he-man Torontonian to be interested in the theatre or art or poetry."

If that wasn't the kind of quip likely to endear him to locals reading it over their morning coffee, or indeed, likely to encourage them to come see the show, there was more where that came from.

"In Hamilton (Ontario) I tried to pay for a drink with a US dollar and the man wouldn't have it. I told him I'd met some strange people in my time, including a Frenchman in Paris who fell in love with the Eiffel Tower but he was unique. The city fathers ought to make him their main tourist attraction. 'Roll up, roll up,' says I, 'and see the only man in the world who refused an American dollar.' The New York Tourist board should spend a free weekend in Toronto obtaining a few pointers on how not to attract tourists."

The clincher might have been this bon mot. "At one particularly low point in my life, I thought of coming to the new world to be a house painter. I must have been out of my mind or drinking poor stuff at the time."

That low point should have been in stark contrast to where he was now. He'd come to Canada to work as conferencier of a jazz revue, a job for which Art Cohen was reportedly paying him $3000 per week. That was just less than the average Torontonian took him home in a year. For that money, his task was to MC this star-studded bill that included Nina Simone, jazz saxophonist Gerry Mulligan, Oscar Brown Jnr. (a singer whose songs espoused black freedom), legendary African drummer Babatunde Olatunji, interpretative dancer Carmen de Lavallade, and renowned trumpeter Maynard Ferguson.

It was quite a collection of talent yet Behan's presence at the centre of it struck some observers as odd.

"The idea makes as much sense," wrote The Toronto Star, "as importing Louis Armstrong to Dublin to chair a discussion by Irish antiquarians of the Gaelic epic poem Táin Bó Cúailnge and its legendary hero, Cúchulainn."

Yet, such was Cohen's confidence in the enterprise, that, even before a note had been played in Toronto, there were ads in the New York papers promoting its scheduled April 1st debut at the Royale Theatre on Broadway. While the musical acts made some sense as a package, there were legitimate questions about the validity or suitability of Behan as the man keeping the show on the road each evening.

"In spite of the signals I'm getting from the sidelines, we're not sure how things are going to go," admitted Behan after rehearsals. "I am supposed to interrupt and explain the universality and catholic quality of jazz. There are some Africans in the show and at one point I talk to the drum. I make some remarks and I may knock Canada a few times. I think it is not a bad place for other people. The performers have a lot of fun and Ferguson will send the people who know jazz. What I am supposed to do is explain to the ordinary people that every time Louis Armstrong blows a trumpet, God does not appear at the other end."

If that was a case of damning a show with faint praise, he was even more blunt about its chances of success in private.

"The show's a lemon," he told Eamonn Martin. "I don't know what to do. I've signed the contract. I've got to go on stage. But I can't go on stage with a show like that."

Before the show kicked off, Behan, and Babatunde Olatunji, the lead drummer from "Impulse", were on "Fighting Words", a Canadian talk show hosted by Nathan Cohen, Their fellow panellists were Morley Callaghan, a Canadian writer, and Claude Dewhurst, former Chief of the British Mission to the Soviet Forces in East Germany. The format consisted of Cohen throwing out quotes for the guests to debate. He opened the discussion with a statement from Lord Beaverbrook that,

"There are countries so underdeveloped today that the gift of independence is like the gift of a razor to a child."

That divided the quartet nicely and Behan was soon at verbal loggerheads with Dewhurst, in particular, about imperialism and, of course, the English influence on countries like Ireland and India. Speaking well, he delivered a telling anecdote about the British Army's massacre of Indians at Amritsar in 1919. Then, Cohen upped the ante, starting the next debate with a quote from Heywood Broun: "The Irish are the cry-babies of the western world." Behan didn't rise to the bait, instead referencing Otto Von Bismarck's line, "If the Dutch had Ireland it would be a garden, if the Irish had Holland, they would all drown."

That appearance helped to publicise the show, and, on the opening night of the production, Behan lived up to the publicity material advertising him as "a combination of master of ceremonies-storyteller-act introducer!" He played the flute, sang an Irish song to African drum accompaniment, and did a number from "The Hostage", from which he also quoted liberally during his ad-libs. Unfortunately for Cohen, much of what he was saying was inaudible to a crowd whose ears were not tuned to the Dublin accent, most especially when the words were being drunkenly slurred. The Ottawa Citizen put it politely when it said he "occasionally acted as master of ceremonies".

As the person closest to him testified, it was much, much worse than that.

"His personality was swallowed by the arena and the hours he spent drinking made him mumble his lines," wrote Beatrice. "This was Punchinello, not Brendan Behan. Long before the performance ended I knew it was a disaster. My husband, the writer, was making a fool of himself for a couple of thousand dollars. It was a cruel dissipation of his talent."

The on-stage debacle gave birth to an off-stage performance the headlines from which dwarfed the coverage of the show. After the debut at the O'Keefe Centre on Tuesday night, March 21st, the Behan party repaired to the Barclay Hotel where a trio of musicians were playing the Oasis Room. Without being asked or requesting permission, as was his usual style, he turned the ensemble into a quartet, a move that drew boos from the rest of the patrons, an attempt to silence him by the MC Bob Rose, and a cameo which culminated in him breaking the leg of a piano.

"Somebody heckled him and that's when the Irish stew hit the fan," the Club Oasis maître d' told a local gossip columnist. "I've never seen or read any of his plays but I want to tell you his nightclub ad-libs can be about as ripe as they come. Before somebody got hurt, I doused the lights, and eventually he sailed out, singing the Jewish national anthem. I hope I never have to find out what he does for an encore."

The encounter with the instrument was only the preliminary bout. Upon returning to the York Hotel, Behan was thirsty for more drink. When the night porter informed him that the city's liquor laws prevented him from serving any, he, predictably enough, went ballistic. "I'm not moving 'til I get a fucking drink!"

He was as good as his word. His belligerence inevitably causing a fracas in which John Matthews, a hotel security officer, incurred a black eye for his troubles. Even still, the staff seemed determined to keep the matter in-house. A number of them got together to bundle him upstairs and into his room, perhaps believing that once the door was shut and the beast contained, some sort of sanity might prevail.

"If you don't keep that man in his room," security warned Beatrice, who trailed behind them, "we'll have him arrested."

Once back in the room, Behan began phoning reception, demanding drink be delivered to him.

"It was late when we got back to our hotel," wrote Beatrice. "In Dublin it's not unusual for hotel guests to drink until the small hours in the lobby but Toronto is a conservative city. The only reason Brendan had come to Toronto was for the money and, since he spent his money as soon as he made it, I couldn't see the point of the visit. Now he didn't want to go to bed."

When his initial threats failed, he pleaded with the receptionists down the phone to get him drink. Eventually, somebody in management made the executive decision to shut off power to the elevator in case he tried to make good on promises to come down and sort them out. Shortly before dawn, the police were called. Officers David Percy and Ronald Lang were first on the scene, getting about ten feet from the door to Behan's room when he emerged.

"Who the hell are you?" he roared.

They introduced themselves and when Behan recognised Percy's Irish accent, he delivered a torrent of abuse, calling him, amongst many other things, "a dirty Irish bastard!" Hotel staff later testified he was "charging around the corridors like a wild, naked bull". It took reinforcements and the arrival, in particular of Detective Edward Trevelyan (reputed to be the toughest man on the Toronto force), to put a stop to his gallop.

"He thinks he's a strong man but there's not much muscle," said Trevelyan, as he recounted how he and his colleagues subdued Behan and took him into custody.

"I sat on the bed, powerless to move, listening to the wild and unnecessary scene outside my door," wrote Beatrice. "Nothing had gone right since we arrived in Canada. Toronto didn't appeal to me; it lacked the friendliness of New York; its people were reserved. I cried as I thought of Brendan locked once again in a police cell. I wanted to be out of Toronto, just as I wanted

Brendan to be with me. Am I losing control of him? I asked myself. I hadn't his constitution which could soak up punishment, nor his ability to sneer at adversity. I was close to despair."

Behan spent five and a half hours in the holding cells at Regent's Street Police Station. When the time came for him to leave for court next morning, he bamboozled the officers in charge by speaking Irish to them, then he emptied his pockets of any cash and handed the money to his fellow prisoners. With the newspaper cameras capturing the moment, he did the perp walk while handcuffed to a policeman. Upon arriving in court, he introduced himself to the other four ne'er do wells awaiting the judge, and by the time he stood in front of Magistrate Donald Graham, it was obvious to onlookers that Behan, for once wearing a tie, had a cut on the bridge of his nose from the previous night's quarrel.

"You just don't get used to these things," Beatrice told a reporter who approached her as she ate breakfast at the hotel that morning. "Naturally I'm worried. In Dublin it takes only 10 minutes to get something like this straightened out. I don't know how long it will take here."

He was charged with two counts of assault – one against a policeman (he did manage to land a blow on Trevelyan's head), and one count of causing a disturbance. Joseph Sedgwick, a lawyer sent by Cohen to represent his "conferencier", told the judge he knew nothing of the case and asked for his client to be remanded on bail for a week. Although Crown Counsel JB Galbraith suggested no bail should be granted, Magistrate Graham remanded him on bail of $500 for one week.

"On Monday, Mayor Nathan Phillips gave me a pair of gold cufflinks," Behan told reporters outside the court. "And on Wednesday they gave me a pair of steel handcuffs. I wonder which of these is the proper credentials for a writer? The cufflinks are an honour. The handcuffs show I' m not a statue yet."

As that comment suggested, he was in jovial form. When asked about having to return to Toronto for his next court appearance, he quipped: "I have a pressing engagement with the representative of the Queen of England."

He was due back on stage at the O'Keefe Center for the matinee performance that afternoon, March 22nd but Behan had other things on his mind. Well, one thing. He headed to the pub and embarked on a two-day skite that included getting up on stage at the Walker House Hotel and singing with the band. If the people there were more tolerant of his efforts than at the Oasis Room, his producer's patience was being tested to breaking point.

Before the curtain came up on the matinee of Impulse, Cohen walked onto the stage at the O'Keefe Center and told the audience that Behan would not be appearing because he was indisposed. Such was his standing on this illustrious bill that Cohen advised any patrons disappointed by the Irishman's absence they would be refunded the price of their tickets at the box office. Only 12 took him up on the offer but the fact there were just over 200 others present in the 3100 seat arena suggested Cohen's ambitious concoction of a show was already in serious trouble.

"After I bailed him out, he gave me his word, 'I'll be there, I'll not let you down,'" said Cohen. "But he didn't show up. The problem is a personal one. Mr. Behan is a great writer and a great artist. As far as I'm concerned his conduct in the theatre is thoroughly professional. The show is interesting and special. It will open on Broadway on schedule."

That night, just under a thousand turned up to see "Impulse", and again, only a handful walked back out when they learned Behan was absent. Still, the writing was on the wall for what was ultimately an ill-conceived production.

"I agree with the critics that it lacks cohesion," said Cohen, announcing his decision to cancel the show and to abandon the transfer to New York. "All the artists are good, individually. Naturally, I'm disappointed. But I think the first thing a professional does is appraise the problems and act accordingly. I don't think this show is good enough for Broadway. Brendan Behan hasn't helped matters much."

Of course, Behan was oblivious to all this. He was in mid-binge and, anyway, soon had far more important matters to contend with than losing an admittedly highly-paid gig. Beatrice finally caught up with him in a bar and she had a plan of action in place to try to stop the madness. She wanted him to check in to a private hospital in Sunnyside, a facility recommended to her by Dr. Carmel McKenna, sister of Petronella O'Flanagan, an Irish journalist based in Toronto. Inevitably, the idea didn't appeal to him but when his wife persisted, he finally relented, "All right then."

Later, they concluded that his lack of resistance was a sign of just how physically sick he was. His old friend Eamonn Martin drove the couple to the hospital and almost as soon as arriving, Behan lapsed into a diabetic coma. He had been diagnosed with a mild form of diabetes by Dr. Rory Childers back in 1957. When another physician advised him to always carry a couple of lumps of sugar in his jacket, Behan asked: "Is that in case I should meet a horse?" For all the humour he knocked out of it, this condition was not conducive to the hard-drinking life.

"Mrs, Behan, your husband is very ill," said Dr. David W. Pratt after examining the patient. "I'm afraid he might die."

This was the grim reality of the situation as Beatrice and Martin kept vigil and, inevitably, they were too preoccupied by his condition to worry about his outstanding legal commitments. When he failed to appear in court on March 27th, Judge Donald Graham issued a bench warrant for his arrest, declared the bail money forfeited, and ordered a member of the Toronto constabulary to be stationed outside his room in the hospital.

"Each day I sat by the bedside in the hospital," wrote Beatrice Behan. "In his grey, strained face his eyes were dark and sunken. He wasn't able to talk to me. But, after about a week, he was able to sit up on his pillows. I didn't dare tell him that outside his door, a detective sat keeping watching on him. Surely, I asked myself, the police must know or have been told, how ill he is. Did they imagine he was feigning illness and might attempt to run away?"

The severity of his health problems brought such intense newspaper interest that somebody said the Canadian media hadn't been this frenzied since the Boyd Gang, the most notorious 1940s hoodlums. The coverage prompted headlines like, "One more spree may end it all", "Behan must quit bottle" and "Stay Dry – Or Die! Scared Behan Told". All very accurate representations of the new reality. For a time it seemed he would never rise to embark on another spree. Once he did start to improve, Dr. Pratt was looking beyond the impact of the abuse of alcohol on the patient in his search to explain his patterns of behaviour.

"Can you tell me if your husband ever suffered an injury to his head?" he asked Beatrice one night.

Beatrice recounted the many, many fights in which her husband had been embroiled over the years, told him the stories of physical abuse he'd incurred in Borstal, and mentioned several bad falls he'd had when intoxicated.

"I would like him to undergo neurological testing," said Pratt. "I think there may be pressure on his brain causing him to behave as he does."

If it seemed like an idea worth exploring to Beatrice, Brendan was, of course, of a different mindset. He "objected violently" to the suggestion and once he was on the mend, there was no way to force or cajole him into agreeing. Putting aside her frustration and disappointment at his refusal to go down this new road, Beatrice, nevertheless, continued to fight his cause in the papers.

"It was the strain of work and then suddenly going on the gargle," she said, explaining his collapse to journalists. "I was very concerned about him but he seems much better today. He even managed a joke or two with his doctors and nurses."

Once the severity of his condition became apparent, the Toronto police announced they wouldn't execute the arrest warrant as long as he remained in hospital and was visited only by his wife. Eamonn Martin was reduced to making phone calls.

"I don't think he'll ever drink again," said Martin, relating the details from one of their conversations to the Associated Press. "Brendan was very much improved today. In fact, he was his usual sparkling, witty self except he tires quickly. The man who gives Brendan another drink is a murderer."

After a couple of setbacks, Behan emerged from danger and was soon ready to re-engage with the world. He began walking the corridors of the hospital with the aid of a cane, beseeched a waiter at the Royal York hotel to bring him a plate of his favourite spaghetti, and started to wade through all the letters and telegrams received from well-wishers. He was impressed by how many people in Toronto had been concerned about his welfare. Not impressed enough though.

The lay-off had done little to improve his attitude toward his host country. Even from his hospital bed, he was able to create controversy and garner headlines, something that said as much about his abrasive personality as it did about the now insatiable appetite of the local papers for Behan stories.

"I don't want anything I have written to be on the CBC (Canadian Broadcasting Company) or on stage or sold in bookshops in Canada," said Behan in an interview conducted at his bedside in Sunnyside Hospital. "I want to get away from the Toronto Sabbath which is 50 per cent bootlegging."

Declaring his visit one big mistake and deriding Canada as "a little country", Behan claimed to have called the CBC to demand they not show a film version of "The Quare Fellow" that was scheduled to be broadcast a few weeks later. The CBC responded to reporters' questions about the matter by pointing out Behan would have to take legal action to force the withdrawal of the programme. The small print didn't matter so much. He was just spoiling for a fight.

When photographers came calling, he was only happy to oblige them. He posed for one shot, wearing pyjamas, with a thick cigar in between his fingers. In another, he had on an elaborate Indian headdress and the report beneath claimed he'd purchased it from the Iroquois Indians at Brantford Reserve. Nobody forced him to sit for the cameras for those shots but when he saw the subsequent pictures in the papers, he was up in arms. Some of his anger was justified. One of the American papers dubbed him "Chief Firewater" and claimed he'd asked to become a blood brother of the Iroquois.

The truth was rather more mundane. Martin said the traditional war-bonnet had been brought along to Behan's room by a photographer who gave it to the patient as a gift, after first taking a few photographs of him wearing it. These pictures then turned up in newspapers across America over the next few days. A classic paparazzi money-making sting. In another shot that made it big on the wires, Behan was captured, sitting up in bed, with his hands clasped together and a solemn look on his face, praying, or least appearing to pray for the cameras. Unable perhaps to resist the limelight and desperate for the oxygen of celebrity, he even conducted a television interview from his hospital room.

"I'm like Lazarus returning from the dead," said Behan. "I have made a humble resurrection."

That much, at least, was true.

CHAPTER TEN

California
Here He Comes

How does one equate the bumptious Brendan with the fair and faultless Beatrice? For one thing it is obvious that she respects her husband and his work, and for another, she is concerned with his health and well-being. It is not generally known that Behan suffers from both diabetes and a liver disorder. In short, alcohol is poison to Behan. Even in my bleared condition I saw that Mrs. Behan knew how to handle Brendan. She ministered to him with consummate skill and never once became a shrew or scold. To have won the devotion of a well-bred and intelligent woman, Behan cannot be the web-footed hod carrier he often appears to be.

SWANK MAGAZINE, MAY, 1961

ON 12 April, 1961, Yuri Gagarin became the first man to travel into space and to complete a circumnavigation of earth. The world was astonished and impressed when news broke that the Soviet Air Force pilot had flown Vostok 1 at speeds of 17,000 miles per hour. For America, there was also the matter of the Russians stealing a march in terms of space technology and striking a propaganda blow in the Cold War. In Sunnyside hospital in Toronto, a fellow patient recognised the momentous event as a chance to tweak Brendan Behan, a man who was always trumpeting the greatness of the United States to his Canadian hosts.

"Well, Behan," asked the Canadian, "what do you think of your Yanks now?"

"I'm not a Yank and you're not a Russian," said Behan. "You're a Canadian so stick to your league – ice hockey."

The following day, Behan was released from hospital; a spokesman for the institution saying he was "all dried out" after 16 days in bed and, what they called, "two alcoholic seizures". Upon leaving Sunnyside, he went straight to Toronto City Hall detective bureau to surrender to the authorities. During a ten-minute court appearance, Dr. Pratt testified he needed further treatment and he was bailed on a bond of $1000. On April 27th, he was back before Justice Donald Graham, evincing his usual lack of irreverence for the legal system.

"This is no time to talk to the magistrate about Socrates," Behan whispered to his lawyer when he got involved in a philosophical discussion with the judge. "The magistrate is anxious to get on to the next drunk case and then, I'm sure to go get a drink himself."

The magistrate wasn't taking matters as lightly as the defendant.

"The accused is a very sick man," said Graham before imposing a fine of $200. "I have no intention of making a martyr out of him. He should know what happens when he takes a drink – he goes berserk."

Sauntering out of court, making a V for victory sign for the cameras, Behan didn't exactly cut a contrite figure as he dismissed the size of the fine. "Money is only a relative thing. I've never had it and I don't want it."

As for the Canadian justice system, he was hopeful. "The judge acted like a judge, not a Toronto judge."

That was as matter of fact as he got that day. Everything else was designed to entertain the hacks and drive up the column inches. As to why the authorities had pressed on with the case against him, he could only think of one reason.

"In 1867, there was a Fenian raid on Canada, and my grandfather was on it. But that's quite a way back to carry a grudge."

Behan In The USA

'I am a drinker with a writing problem': Brendan Behan at Dublin Airport before he flies out for a Broadway production of 'The Hostage'.
EVENING HERALD

PLAYBILL

Cort
Theatre

a weekly magazine for theatregoers

THE
HOSTAGE

Start spreading the news: Brendan Behan gives a reading at the 8th Street Bookshop, New York on October 13, 1960.
GETTY IMAGES

Inset left: The November 1960 edition of Broadway magazine 'Playbill' featuring Behan on the cover.

Home, sweet home: Behan steps off a Cunard liner in Cobh (above) for a trip home in December, 1960.
IRISH EXAMINER/EVENING ECHO

My love: Behan with his wife Beatrice (left) in New York.

The quare fellow: Behan turns on the Christmas lights in Dublin in 1959 (right).
IRISH INDEPENDENT

Neighbourly love: Behan receives the key to Jersey City from Mayor Charles Witkowski, after the playwright was banned from marching in the New York St. Patrick's Day parade.
BETTMANN/CORBIS

He gets my vote: Behan at the Democratic Party headquarters on US presidency election night in November 1960.
GETTY IMAGES

Force of nature: Behan is arrested in Toronto in March 1961.
GETTY IMAGES

In loving memory: The plaque erected outside the Hotel Chelsea, the last place Behan lived in New York.

Along the banks of the Royal Canal: The Brendan Behan statue in Dublin. **Inset:** A self-portrait which featured in the February '62 edition of 'Esquire'.

One reporter complimented him on being free of prejudice.

"That's not true," said Behan. "but I have so many prejudices they cancel each other out! I guess I'm the antidote to Dale Carnegie."

There were some parting shots about the host country.

"Canada is barbaric without being picturesque. When you're in jail in Canada, how can you tell the difference? Canada has everything – drug addiction, juvenile delinquency. New York is my Lourdes. I go there for spiritual replenishment. I'm so glad to leave that even seeing the Howard Johnson hotel architecture in Buffalo cheers me up."

By the time he returned to New York, he was back bending the ear of Leonard Lyons about his love for his adopted city.

"Frankly, the only space I'm interested in for the rest of my life is that space between the statues of Father Duffy and George M. Cohan (both in Times Square). New York is the only true city. In London, the only ones on the street after midnight are criminals and cops. In New York at 3am, you can see people on 42nd Street who'd be picked up even in Paris' Latin Quarter."

Who could blame him for the affection when Manhattan was offering him so many opportunities When Bernard Geis published "Harpo Speaks", the autobiography of Harpo Marx, the party to celebrate the launch was at the Algonquin Hotel, and Behan, of course, was an invited guest. This was the kind of company he exulted in. These were men he'd grown up watching at the cinema and after being introduced to Groucho Marx during his previous stay in New York, the pair had ended up talking about "Finnegan's Wake". This time around, he found himself travelling down in the elevator with another of the Marx Brothers.

"Once we were making a movie called 'A Night at the Opera'," said Harpo before Behan interrupted.

"That's like Leonardo da Vinci saying, 'Once I was painting a picture called the Last Supper.'"

At the party, somebody gave Behan a horn so, like any student of the Marx Brothers' oeuvre would, he honked in Harpo's ear to get him to pull one of his famous reaction faces for the cameras.

"He's unique," Behan told one reporter of Harpo. "He's a Presbyterian Eskimo."

Even now, almost a year after first touching down in America and realising the extent of his own celebrity, proximity to his heroes could still bring out child-like enthusiasm in Behan.

"We had a great party in New York, and Harpo and I were televised and photographed all over the place wearing Harpo wigs," he wrote to his half-brother Rory. "It was in the papers all over but I don't suppose the Dublin papers had it – they only seem to know when I'm in jail or dying."

If the Marx Brothers had made their last movie in 1949, more contemporary acts were fond of Behan too. Having sold more than a million copies of their comedy album "2000 years with Mel Brooks and Carl Reiner", Reiner, one half of the hottest comic duo in America, invited him along to the New York studio where they were recording the follow-up, "2,000 and One Years with Carl Reiner and Mel Brooks" before a live audience. At one point in a skit, Reiner asked Brooks (playing the 2000 year old man) if there were such a thing as national anthems when he was born.

"Yeah, every cave had a national anthem," said Brooks before launching into a song called, 'Let them all go to hell, except Cave 76'.

On the album, Behan can be clearly heard guffawing in the background. After the session ended, he went up to Brooks and Reiner.

"You know, I've got a new motto now," he said before delivering a line in Irish.

"What does that mean?" asked Reiner.

"Let 'em all go to hell, except Cave 76."

Not everything went swimmingly on his return to New York. He still had the uncanny knack for finding trouble in the oddest places. "Gone with the Wind" had just been re-released to coincide with the 100th anniversary of the Civil War. Behan ended up going along to a showing where, he soon discovered, he was sitting behind a tourist from Ohio. When it came to the scene in which Atlanta is set aflame, Behan started to applaud, a little too enthusiastically. His "friend" from Ohio, turned around and punched him in the face.

"I'm puzzled why he did that," said Behan, recounting the tale later. "Even with a strong wind behind it, no fire from Atlanta could possibly ever reach Ohio."

After a brief respite in New York, he was on the move again. After finishing on Broadway, Littlewood's production of "The Hostage" had gone on a North American tour and following successful stints in Toronto, Montreal, Chicago, Philadelphia and Los Angeles, there was to be one final stop in San Francisco. The playwright wanted to be there to meet the cast on the last leg of their journey with his play but Beatrice, still nervous of airplanes, refused to fly across the country. So, showing his usual chivalry, he told her to follow by train and assured her he'd pick her up at the station when she arrived on the west coast.

"Do ye suppose they'll stage an earthquake for me while I'm here?" he asked reporters when he touched down in San Francisco on April 30th, 1961. "Most people talk about San Francisco like the Irish talk about Lourdes."

He declared his desire to meet the writer Jack London, warned that there would be no attempt at moral uplift in his play, and cautioned that although he was on the dry, he was hoping for a special dispensation to have a dozen Irish coffees while he was there. Certainly, the town was to his liking. When they drove up Kearney Street for the first time that day, he told his companions, "Look at all the bail bondsmen. I'm going to love this city."

The cast of "The Hostage" hadn't seen Behan since the show left New York. But, as they traversed the country, they kept up with his latest antics in the newspapers of every city they visited. Now that he was back in the fold, those members of the cast who'd replaced some of the original performers along the way were about to see a lot more of him than some of them expected. Not long after the curtain went up at the Geary Theatre on opening night, May 2nd, Behan appeared from the wings and strode across the stage.

"Ladies and gentlemen," he slurred, "I represent culture."

"Culture?" shouted a voice from the front row. "Hell, he's just a sloppy drunk."

That he may have been, but some in the audience had come along just to see if the writer became part of the action. They applauded his appearance and laughed at his attempt to humour them, especially when he took a bottle of beer off a table and started to try to sprinkle the crowd with it.

"Every performance while Brendan's in town is nerve-wracking," said one actor afterwards. "You never know when he's going to pop in."

Some were more open with their dissension.

"He may be a very sick man but it does leave one in a damn awkward position to be cut off in the middle of a speech while he makes a fool of himself in front of the audience," said Beaulah Garrick, now playing Miss Gilchrist.

The veterans, of course, were a little more sanguine about the whole business. Eileen Kenneally had first witnessed his unexpected, on-stage cabaret during the original production in London. So, the sight of him appearing in a nun's habit while smoking a cigar and doing a Groucho Marx impression, as he did later in the San Francisco run, wasn't going to faze her much.

"It's his play and he is the play so whether or not he interrupts the action, it doesn't change the meaning," said Kenneally. "There's an Irish folk dance called the Black Bird that he often does impromptu on stage. Incidentally, he's very good at it."

After his opening night cameo, Behan left the stage and headed across the street to the Curtain Call bar where the press photographers caught up with him so they had pictures to go with the story of his latest drunken onstage exploit. Leonard Lyons phoned from New York to ask him what had happened. He said he was only in the bar to enlist members for his new organisation, TWA, the Teetotal Writers' Association. He also lamented to his friend that his looks, his missing teeth and his unkempt hair meant people just assumed he was drunk even when he was sober.

A lame enough case for the defence, especially when the first thing Milton Machlin, an American author and an old friend from Paris, noticed in Behan's hotel room, was an ice box full of Cordon Rouge. Not to mention the scenes witnessed one evening by journalist Herb Caen in the Geary Cellar, the bar underneath the theatre. As the play was going down a storm upstairs, Behan was ordering big.

"Four bottles of champagne – French Brut," he barked at the waitress.

"No, no, you mustn't drink," said a young woman nearby.

"All right, all right, a round of 7-Up," he said, suddenly acquiescing.

By the time the drink was served though, he'd changed course again.

"Make mine a cognac – Remy Martin," he shouted. Once that

arrived, he downed it in one gulp and then went back upstairs to interrupt the show.

"At Ondine's Yacht Dock the following morning, consumed with high spirits and low champagne, Behan felt the urge to go swimming, and to the assorted gasps of onlookers, he ripped off his clothes and started to dive into the bay," wrote Caen in the Los Angeles Times. "Cooler heads prevailed. An even cooler head might suggest he buy underwear."

He was in the throes of what would later be described as "a four-day champagne binge" in a city where his arrival had been eagerly anticipated. Indeed, when he visited San Francisco's storied City Lights bookstore around midnight one evening, word quickly got around that a literary celebrity was in their midst. Before long, he had an audience hanging on his every word in a corner of the shop.

Months before he ever set foot in San Francisco, Enrico Banducci, owner of The Hungry i, the hippest nightclub in North Beach, had told reporters he'd made Behan a standing offer of $1,000 to do a week of shows at his place. As it happened, his arrival in town coincided with Banducci going to jail for contempt of court. Upon his release, there was a protest march and, of course, Behan lent his weight to the cause, marching through the streets behind the victim of injustice. When everybody involved ended up back at The Hungry i that night, Behan threw himself into the festivities.

As she sat on a train winding its way across America, Beatrice hoped the scare in Toronto might have brought her husband to his senses. She hoped in vain. It had had just the opposite effect.

"From the beginning, Beatrice had been against Brendan's return to the States," wrote Rae Jeffs, his editor in London. "Now that he was drinking again, she became even more so and accompanied him knowing full well that, in a country which encouraged him to publicise a false version of himself, the task of reminding him he was not a tin god was going to be twice as difficult. I do not intend to enlarge in detail on the events of his second trip, except to mark it chronologically as the end of Brendan as his true friends enjoyed him."

When Beatrice alighted at San Francisco, there was nobody there to greet her. A bad sign that prefaced worse. Upon reaching The Clift Hotel where her husband was billeted, she found him unconscious, in a room reeking of stale air, strewn with champagne bottles and carpeted with unopened letters and telegrams.

"I looked at his inert, shirt-clad figure sprawled across the crumpled bed," wrote Beatrice. "His unshaven face was puffed and yellow. He must have been drinking himself into a coma for days. By now I knew not to hesitate, even though he might regain consciousness and pretend he was fit. There was no point any longer in quarrelling with him about his escapades. My only concern was to get him out of this fetid hotel room and into hospital."

Jim McGuinness, a former Curragh internee who'd once given Behan his own column in the Irish Press, was then working as a journalist in San Francisco. In the pile of letters on the floor, Beatrice found a sheet on which McGuinness had left a phone number. She called him in a panic. He put her in touch with a Dr. Traynor and Behan ended up in St. Mary's on Hayes Street. Over a century earlier, a contingent from the Sisters of Mercy in Ireland had come to San Francisco and built it as the first Catholic hospital in the city. When Behan arrived there, many of the nurses were still Irish-born and inevitably disposed to looking after the star patient.

"Brendan is in good form, but it's a good idea to have him spend three or four days in hospital – whatever the doctors say," said Beatrice to reporters. Back at the hotel, she received anonymous calls from Irish-Americans telling her to get her drunken bum of a husband out of the city.

Once he emerged from the diabetic coma, Behan went, in the usual way, rather quickly from death's door to the front door. "I feel smashing," he said. He also promised to lay off the drink and soon he was cutting a more refined figure in public. On May 9th, he attended a Press Club luncheon where the speaker was Mrs. Elizabeth R. Smith, the Secretary of the Treasury in the United States, a woman whose signature appeared on all legal tender notes in America. Of course, the pair were introduced. He asked her to autograph a dollar bill and she did so, cautioning him, "Spend it wisely".

At that event, he sipped water throughout despite several people offering him whiskey, scotch and all other manner of liquor. But, the sobriety didn't hold. He went back drinking soon enough, punctuating the renewed binge with cameos on stage at the Geary Theatre during the show. One night, he was blessing the characters of Mr. Mulleady and Miss Gilchrist in flawless (if slurred) Latin, the next he was standing around pretending to be one of the tenants of the Dublin boarding-house in the play.

The press catalogued every drunken step he took. There were plenty of reporters in tow when he made a pilgrimage to the No Name bar in Sausalito, a countercultural hotspot in a community of the same. Charles Gould was the barman on duty when Behan swung through with his entourage and after observing him up-close, he travelled into San Francisco to see the show on a night when, inevitably, Behan delivered an unscripted monologue. Afterwards, he plucked up the courage to speak to Behan.

"Behan was drinking champagne from a tumbler and singing what Gould called 'dirty songs'," wrote Michael O'Sullivan. "He approached Behan to congratulate him. All

Behan wanted to know was if Gould thought he looked 'soused' when he made his speech from the stage, to which he replied, 'just about as soused as you are now.' When the bar's patrons and the attendant reporters began to draw away from the swaggering, staggering drunk, Gould was struck by the pathos of the moment."

On May 13, the last night of its stint at the Geary Theatre, "The Hostage" received a lengthy ovation that culminated in Behan dancing the Black Bird on the stage, much to the delight of most of the audience. Since this was the end of a journey which, for some of the cast and crew, had begun the previous September in New York, the after-party was long and lavish. Steaks and burgundy were consumed and a sing-song broke out. Among those in attendance that evening was an attractive 21 year old Dubliner named Valerie Danby-Smith.

"Her creamy complexion, pink cheeks and tangled dark hair," wrote Bernice Kert of Danby-Smith one time, "reminded some people of Goya's Duchess of Alba".

When he spoke at the James Joyce Society at the Gotham Book Mart the previous November, Behan had mentioned Danby-Smith to his audience. By then, she was staying at the Algonquin and was formally employed as a sort of secretary or, as she put it herself, "general dogsbody", among whose duties were typing up bits of "Richard's Cork Leg" and handling the constant requests for interviews. If very few people would have been up to that task, it was a role for which she had unique qualifications. Despite her youth, Danby-Smith came with a resume like few others.

In early 1959, the then 18 year old decided to leave Dublin for Spain. She started dabbling in journalism and was dispatched to try to get an interview with Ernest Hemingway at the Hotel Suecia in Madrid. Hemingway was back in the country for the first time since the Spanish Civil War, writing an essay about bullfighting for LIFE magazine. She managed to get a sit-down with the great man, and even if it didn't go as well as she might have hoped from a journalistic point of view, it marked the start of a grand adventure.

Hemingway offered a job as his assistant. The pay was $250 per month (about ten times her freelance journalism income), all meals paid for, and the opportunity to be an eyewitness to literary history. That summer, Danby-Smith travelled through Spain and France as part of his cuadrilla (entourage). The presence of an attractive young woman in his orbit prompted speculation about the nature of their relationship. Although there seems no question the 61 year old Hemingway liked having her around, some observers felt he was infatuated with the Dubliner. For her part, Danby-Smith preferred to see herself as a "muse", and described his treatment of her as fatherly.

Hemingway invited Danby-Smith to travel to Cuba to continue working for him. She returned to Dublin en route to Havana where she called into the Behans' house on Anglesea Road. She had first met Brendan when he'd visited the hotel in Enniskerry, County Wicklow where Danby-Smith spent much of her childhood. Now, she was bringing news to him that Hemingway had read and enjoyed "Borstal Boy". She also told him of her plans to move to Cuba and he hit her with a counter-offer of employment.

"Why in the name of Jaysus would you want to work for America's greatest writer when you could work for Ireland's best instead?" asked Behan. "I can easily get you a job with 'The Hostage' company. Forget about the ol' man and Cuba, and support one of your own."

After spending much of 1960 with Hemingway whose health, physical and mental, was in decline, Danby-Smith bade him a tearful farewell, and made a brief stop in Dublin before flying to New York to take Behan up on his job offer. She arrived at the Algonquin in mid-October, her suitcases bulging with letters and gifts that friends of the Behans had asked her to bring over from Ireland. Brendan was in the lobby and bellowed, "A cailin mo chroi" when he saw her.

"Fame had not changed his countenance, with its mischievous sky-blue eyes, ruddy complexion and decidedly crooked nose," wrote Danby-Smith. "The jet-black curly hair remained unruly. He wore his habitual starched white dress shirt with long sleeves and open collar and navy woollen trousers held up with a pair of braces. His worn brown shoes were vaguely polished."

When Brendan left the Algonquin for Montreal and then Ireland, Danby-Smith stayed on in New York. She found work as a researcher at Newsweek magazine, and having just turned 21, she flew to San Francisco for a weekend to meet up with the Behans. Having enjoyed the party to celebrate the end of "The Hostage", she returned to her room at the Mark Hopkins Hotel.

"I was awakened a short while later when Brendan let himself into my room with a key he must have acquired when he made my hotel reservation," wrote Danby-Smith in her memoir. "I learned then that the romantic fantasies he had hinted at during the preceding months were not just attempts at lighthearted flirtation. It was a night that would change my life forever."

CHAPTER ELEVEN

Brendan Goes
To Hollywood

*One day he picked up a novelty, a magazine devoted to
homosexuals, featuring nude "studies" of handsome young male
models. Brendan pretended to be astonished and shocked by this
publication. To the kiosk attendant, he said, with a show of
indignation: "Who would be buying a rag like this?" The
attendant gave Brendan a sour look and replied: "People like
you." Brendan was delighted with the quickness and accuracy of
the reply. "Begod, you have me there!" he said. "Where can I take
out a lifetime subscription?"*

BRENDAN GILL

TOWARDS the end of the run in San Francisco, the stage
manager Bernie Pollock told Brendan that he and Beulah
Garrick (Mrs. Gilchrist) intended to head down to Los Angeles
once the show was over. Given that Pollock and Garrick had
marriage in mind, they probably didn't expect Behan to ask if
he could tag along. When he announced his intention to do just
that, Beatrice implored him not to. But, how could he resist? Los
Angeles meant Hollywood. So, the night before their scheduled
departure, he persuaded Pollock and the even more reluctant
Garrick that there was room for another couple in the car.

The journey down the Pacific Coast from San Francisco to
Los Angeles in the middle of May, 1961 was memorable for all
the right reasons. There was no drinking and no tantrums, just
a world of wonders to behold. As Bernie drove, Behan sat in the
front seat taking in the often spectacular view of Big Sur, and
offering a comprehensive, improvised and betimes scandalous,
alternative version of American history. In the backseat,

Beatrice and Beulah Garrick enjoyed the show as they cruised highways that took them through and past towns the names of which evoked movies they'd all seen. Santa Barbara. Santa Cruz. Monterey, San Simeon. In Carmel, Brendan stopped because he wanted to post a card from there to his sister Carmel back in Dublin.

When the mood took them, they rolled up to diners to eat and they slept each night in folksy roadside motels. The sun seemed to shine each day and the station wagon mostly shook with laughter. Pollock and Garrick had made Behan promise not to drink, and he'd been as good as his word. Even when Mike Thomas, a journalist with the Monterey Peninsula Herald learned the Irishman was in his town, he found a sober and clear-eyed character, far removed from the cartoonish figure of newspaper legend, sipping mineral water in a restaurant called Neptune's Table, and telling the locals, "It's like paradise down here."

"A good many heads turned to stare at the tousle-haired, rather lumpy, blue-eyed man with the loud, garbled voice which seemed to be saying somewhat shocking but nevertheless entertaining things," wrote Thomas. "Behan's language may be described most delicately as uninhibited, and his decibel count is exceeded only by the astonishing frequency with which certain colourful Anglo-Saxon words recur in his conversation."

Censored for a newspaper audience with dashes replacing swear words, the quotes from the interview often read like something written in code. Witness just one sample.

"I'm a barbarian. I'm open for an offer, though. I could become a fucking south California phony, live on fucking blackstrap molasses and wind up in fucking Forest Lawn."

The idyllic mood of this particular interlude continued even after they reached Los Angeles. There, they checked into the Montecito Hotel perched up high on a hill in Hollywood where Behan quickly became a tourist attraction with his antics in the swimming pool. The keen swimmer could be found each day performing all manner of tricks, half-child on day-release from school, half-performing seal in an aquarium. When he went off the diving board, it was usually while roaring in Irish and very often he came back to the surface minus his trunks.

"I prefer swimming underwater," he said to Mike Kellin, a veteran actor and fellow guest.

"What's stopping you?" asked Kellin.

"What's stopping me is the lack of conversation!" replied Behan.

From his new digs, he found time in between the mischief and devilment to write to his half-brother Rory back in Dublin. He talked about the preferential treatment he received in Frank Sinatra's night club, dubbed the owner of the joint "a tenement aristocrat like myself," compared Sunset Boulevard to Sundrive Road in Crumlin, and name-dropped repeatedly to illustrate the type of celebrities he was now mixing with.

"You will be glad to hear that Fred Astaire got an award here recently and still looks a lean forty," he wrote on May 19th. "We talked about you and me and the Drumcondra cinema and about Waterford City where he went with his wife or someone's wife – they're not too particular about those things (wives, I mean) here – though they don't like bad language as they call it, nor nude bathing – except in the moonlight..."

The day after he penned that, Groucho Marx called to bring him and Beatrice for dinner at the Brown Derby in Hollywood. They dined while discussing James Joyce, and Beatrice found Groucho to be every bit as funny off-screen as he was on it. Eventually, Brendan started listing off the places they'd seen and wanted to see around Los Angeles. He told Marx that he really wanted to see Forest Lawn Cemetery.

"What's your hurry?" quipped the actor.

The honeymoon period in Hollywood came to a rather abrupt end at the pool one day when the newly-engaged Bernie and Beulah (who did later marry) decided they wanted to check out of the hotel and into an apartment. While Beatrice perfectly understood the couple's desire to strike out on their own, Brendan reacted, as his wife put it, like "a spoilt child". Despite reassurances that he'd still get to see Bernie each day, Brendan took the news badly. How badly only became apparent the next day when he disappeared.

Less than 24 hours after the courting couple had checked out of the Montecito, they were back there picking up a desperate Beatrice to go off on a manhunt. Eventually, they found Behan sitting comfortably in a gay bar where the locals were plying him with drink. Of course, finding him was one thing, trying to extricate him from his newfound home from home was something else altogether.

The ever-resourceful Pollock promised him he had champagne back at his apartment, and after the almost obligatory row with a barman about ordering one more for the road, Behan finally agreed to leave. The entourage stopped into a supermarket on Hollywood Boulevard to buy more bubbly – Brendan wanted a dozen bottles, Pollock made him settle for two – and somewhere en route to the Pollock/Garrick apartment, they managed to steer him back to the Montecito. The night fizzled out slowly as the erstwhile stage manager eventually persuaded the playwright it was time for bed.

"We were sorry to see Bernie and Beulah leave Hollywood," remembered Beatrice. "Few men had handled Brendan so coolly and efficiently as Bernie. Now there was only myself to watch over him every day and sometimes he seemed scarcely aware of my presence."

The latter may have been, at least in part, because he was

preoccupied with somebody else, a 27 year old sailor called Peter Arthurs whom he'd met while swimming at the local YMCA. He'd moved his daily swim to the new location after hearing it had an Olympic-sized pool. It was there, while up to his usual horseplay one afternoon, crossing lanes, diving too close to fellow swimmers and generally acting the buffoon, he literally bumped into Arthurs who didn't appreciate this overweight hooligan diving in on top of him as he swam.

"I observed the rowdy little figure as he scrambled up out of the water and took a standing position on the tiled perimeter of the pool's deep end," wrote Arthurs of his first sighting of Behan. "He made a series of attention-compelling hand and head gesticulations. Once this was accomplished, he blessed a half-submerged cadre of laughing idolators with In Nomine Patri and sprinkled their heads with improvised holy water that he scooped up from the pool."

In the dressing-rooms, the pair clashed again. Behan boasted about Jack Paar tormenting him to be a guest on his show; Arthurs responded by mocking him for being a much smaller man that he'd imagined when reading about him in newspapers. After exchanging more insults, the two apparently and, quite bizarrely, decided to become fast friends. Now at some sort of peace, they emerged to find Beatrice in the corridor, sitting on a bench, waiting patiently for her husband. After the obligatory introductions, the trio headed out in to the warmth of a May afternoon in Los Angeles. A riotous visit to the Pickwick Bookstore on the corner of Wilcox Avenue and Hollywood Boulevard where Behan signed autographs for fans was followed by drinks at The Comet, a gay bar, on Cahuenga Avenue.

There, Brendan entertained and appalled the clientele in equal measure. He boasted of his paramilitary career and his lucrative earnings as a writer. Then he sang and danced. Repeatedly. Many of the regulars up and left. Soon, Beatrice and

Arthurs realised the remaining customers were tiring of the Behan show too. They persuaded him to leave and all three headed back to the apartment at the Montecito where Beatrice cooked an enormous meal. Some time after dinner, Behan suggested a swim in the hotel pool. When Arthurs repaired to the bathroom to try on a pair of trunks he was going to borrow, Behan followed him in and the pair had their first sexual encounter.

"A look of pure excitement seeped into his eyes as he continued to fondle my cock and watch it rise to tumescence," remembered Arthurs. "Then with the aid of his free hand, he reached up and opened the mirrored door of the medicine cabinet, then he jerked me off while gleefully observing our reflections in the mirror."

Thus began what was to be a complex relationship that endured on and off over the next two years. A seaman by trade, Arthurs was a native of Dundalk who, after more than a decade traversing the world on ships, had ambitions of becoming an actor. From their unlikely first joust in the YMCA, he would become Behan's confidante, lover, factotum, chauffeur, bodyguard, best friend and worst enemy, depending on the mood and the circumstance. The first test of his loyalty came on May 31st when Behan's antics brought him to the attention of the Los Angeles Police Department.

The evening began quietly enough. Brendan and Beatrice were at M'Goo's Food and Fun, an Irish-themed restaurant on Hollywood Boulevard that attracted tourists with gimmicks such as selling beer by the pound and champagne by the bubble. As had now become something of a pattern, the trouble started when a barman decided Behan had drunk enough and needed to move on.

"Give me a fucking drink!" he roared when hearing he was being cut off.

"You can't use that kind of language in here," said the barman.

"You heard what I said," Behan continued. "Give me a fucking drink."

Matters degenerated from there. The language got more foul, the abuse more intense. Beatrice saw Jerry Brentari, the manager of the restaurant, going for the phone, and knew the arrival of the police was imminent. She tried her best, yet again, to save her husband from himself but there was no persuading him in this mood. Within minutes, she was outside the door watching him being shepherded into the back of a squad car, spouting streams of Irish to the arresting officers who drove him to Precinct 27 in Hollywood. She went back inside, ordered a coffee and considered her options. Bernie Pollock and Beulah had gone to New Mexico. Who now could she call?

By the time she reached Peter Arthurs on the phone, he had already heard about the arrest. It had been a lead item on the radio news bulletins. Indeed, it was such a big story around town that Joe Finnegan, a reporter with UPI, was in the press box at Dodger Stadium covering the Los Angeles Dodgers versus the St. Louis Cardinals that night when his boss called and told him to leave the game and get on the Behan beat. Meanwhile, Arthurs took Beatrice to the International House of Pancakes on Sunset Boulevard as they tried to figure out their next move.

At the police station, Behan refused to toe the line. When Patrolman Charles Brewer tried to take his mug shot, he took a swing at him. Fortunately, he was so drunk he missed.

"He acted like a character out of one of his plays," said Brewer.

If it was theatre, this is where the act took a curious turn. Before Beatrice and Arthurs could do anything to liberate Behan, bail of $325 was posted by somebody called Martin

Bryman. Who was he? Only the proprietor of M'Goos and obviously somebody who subscribed to Behan's own "all publicity is good publicity except your own obituary" mantra.

"He used real foul language – the worst foul language you could possibly hear," said Bryman. "He wanted a drink and we wouldn't serve him. He said he could drink any place he came into. I didn't want him imprisoned, just quietened for a bit."

Shortly after 3am next morning, he was released and, inevitably, gave a virtuoso performance for the reporters gathered at the station house.

"There I was indulging in high spirits, singing a song. And do you know? They arrested me for that. I'm quiet, quiet as a church mouse, now where can we get lager at this hour?"

When the reporters pointed him to a bar, he gave them reams of copy.

On Los Angeles: "Did you ever see a place where people live so far apart? Why should this be unless they hate each other?"

On Russia landing a man in space before America. "I was drinking the bootleg whiskey in Toronto and this man who didn't like Yanks said it was an awful black eye for the Yanks. So I say to him, 'My friend, Ireland will put a shillelagh into orbit, Israel will put a matzo into orbit and Liechtenstein will put a postage stamp into orbit before ever you Canadians put up a mouse.' And do you know what? He hit me just for that, and me a quiet man and all."

On the LAPD: "Fine men all. I was treated fair, fairer than most other places that I temporarily lodged at."

If the quotes weren't stage-Irish enough, he was back at M'Goos that night, drinking with Bryman and dancing for the benefit of reporters. And, in a cameo that demonstrated how intoxicating he found his new celebrity, Behan insisted Arthurs accompanied him to the 24-hour newsstand later that evening so he could buy the freshly-printed newspapers. He read the accounts of his latest travails with a boyish grin on his face. For a man who so often lamented the downside of intrusive fame, he certainly seemed to enjoy a lot of what came with it.

He missed his first court appearance on June 3rd but his lawyer Max Solomon entered not guilty pleas on three misdemeanor charges, and explained his client was busy working on a screenplay. Within a week, the whole matter had been resolved.

"I want to apologise to the people of Los Angeles and your honour for being a nuisance," said Behan to Justice Delbert E. Wong who fined him $250.

The apology made no mention of future behaviour. That was just as well. For Behan and Los Angeles, the party had really just begun and his sudden, outsized media presence meant there was no chance of flying under the radar. Working the early shift at KNX radio in the city one morning early in June, Bob Krane got a call from a listener claiming a man was standing outside on the street, singing and disturbing his sleep. The listener said the man sounded like Brendan Behan because he had "an Irish brogue". He called the police to complain and when they arrived, lo and behold, it was Behan.

Paul Coates was the host of a local television show who was keen to get Behan as a guest. He dispatched one of his team, Irwin Moskowitz, a tee-totaller, to the Montecito to deliver the invite in person. Behan opened the door in his pyjamas, unbuttoned down the front revealing an impressive paunch, and roared at the young man, "Who might you be?" Moskowitz explained his business and he was brought inside. Hours went by. Back at the office, Coates decided to call the hotel. Beatrice answered and put him through to the missing production assistant.

"I think I'm drunk," said Moskowitz. "Mr. Behan made me do it. He told me he'd come on the show if I drank a water glass full of whiskey."

Moskowitz took the rest of the day off work. Behan never did make it to the studio.

"New York has Times Square but Los Angeles is a city with a body but no navel," he told one of the many journalists now queuing up for easy copy. "The only thing I've got against the suburban homes is that they're in the suburbs. The main thing about Hollywood is the number of native Hollywoodsmen you meet. I'm surprised to discover that a lot of people are getting an honest living in these parts."

The natives were thrilled to discover him wherever he went. On a day trip with Arthurs to Marineland of the Pacific, California's first theme park, he was constantly stopped and asked to pose for photographs by people who recognised the celebrity in their midst. Each "fan" was treated to some colourful dialogue, most of which (luckily for them) they struggled to understand but after a while, he complained to his friend, "They'd give you the fucking head-staggers!" Still, he was fascinated by the whales and the sharks and, later waxed lyrical to reporters about how the porpoises were better swimmers than he was.

The press loved this kind of schtick. "I swim like an Irish cop," he said, "stupid but willing."

Even when he was sober, every story seemed to be about drink or at least laced with the stuff.

"I was in Barcelona once for the bullfights but I was too drunk to go," he told the same journalist when announcing plans to head down to Mexico to take in a bullfight.

As in New York, it wasn't just reporters who were interested in him, everybody seemed to want a piece. Columbia Pictures called and offered a cameo appearance in "The Notorious Landlady", a film starring Jack Lemmon, Kim Novak and Astaire. Quite a cast. There was a similar offer of a small role in Jane Fonda's "Walk on the Wild Side".

"I'm a writer, not an actor or anything else that's connected to that bird-brained ilk that is incapable of earning an honest living," said Behan. "Tell them to fuck off."

Desperate to get a break as an actor himself, Arthurs beseeched him to go over to Columbia's lot, hoping such a trip might lead to him being discovered. To no avail. Of course, Behan had been on the radar of some in Hollywood for quite a while. Around the time he was banned from New York's St. Patrick's Day parade earlier in the year, he'd received a letter of solidarity from Jerry Wald. A producer with four Academy Award nominations and an extensive list of credits that included "Peyton Place", Wald's gesture of support also contained a tantalising offer of work.

"I do not believe man's habits and his art should be confused," wrote Wald. "Your talents as a playwright in addition to being Irish seems to make you the ideal man to adapt the work of your fellow countryman James Joyce. Will you consider adapting Ulysses to the big screen?"

Over the previous two years, Wald had presided over adaptions of William Faulkner's "The Sound and the Fury" and D.H. Lawrence's "Sons and Lovers". That he was serious about Behan adapting Joyce can be gleaned from the fact he made several calls to the Montecito, requesting a meeting. Nothing would ever come of the project but that this calibre of people were on his trail demonstrated the standing he enjoyed. Others made offers too.

Sal Mineo, the actor who played Plato in James Dean's "Rebel Without a Cause" and somebody with two Oscar nominations on his CV, wanted Behan to write a screenplay for "Borstal Boy". Mineo was starting a film company with producer Mike Todd Jr. (Elizabeth Taylor's stepson) and the pair thought the book would be the perfect vehicle for their first feature. They made repeated attempts to get Behan to sign up for the project while he was in town.

However, not everybody in Tinseltown was enamoured with the new arrival from Ireland. Peer Oppenheimer, producer of the show "Here's Hollywood", was charged with the task of pre-interviewing Behan for a guest slot. At one point in their conversation, Behan requested that he recite the months of the year. "Why should I?" asked Oppenheimer, reluctant to be part of the inevitable cabaret act. Behan responded by sucker-punching him with an upper cut that split his lip. Before Oppenheimer could retaliate, Arthurs had stepped in and prevented any further blows being exchanged.

That wasn't the end of this particular incident. A few nights later, Oppenheimer was asleep in bed when his phone rang shortly after 2am.

"Where do I find that guy?" shouted Steve McQueen on the other end of the line. "I'm going to smash him!"

"You're going to smash who?" asked Oppenheimer.

"Brendan Behan!" said McQueen, then 32 years old. "I was told he socked you in the face. Nobody is going to beat up a friend of mine and get away with it!"

Wherever he went, havoc surely followed. One morning, the Behans climbed into Arthurs' powder blue Buick and headed south to Mexico. The journey took twice as long as it should have because Brendan insisted on stopping every time he saw something interesting. Which was about every few miles. Then, they were run off the road by a convertible full of teenagers. In a tableau that captured the balance of power in the various relationships, Beatrice and Arthurs pushed the Buick out of the mud as Brendan watched on.

Upon arrival in Tijuana, the trio booked into Caesar's Hotel and Restaurant on Avenida Revolucíon, the preferred destination for Hollywood stars when they crossed the border and an establishment famous for giving the culinary world the Caesar Salad. A city that thrived on its proximity to San Diego and its ability to offer American tourists whatever they fancied that was illegal back home, Behan barely set foot in the room before heading off into the streets to explore. Beatrice and Arthurs gave chase, fearing for his welfare given Tijuana's notoriety for crime and crooked police.

They caught up with him before he could find any serious mischief, all three ending up on the back of a horse and cart with sombreros on their heads, being shaken down for an over-priced tourist photograph by opportunist locals. Later, Brendan embarked on a shopping spree at a Woolworth's, buying a jumper with Aztec designs on it. Before long, the type of reporters who made a living filing copy about the antics of celebrities holidaying in Tijuana caught up with the party in the bar of the Caesar. There, they were treated to a vintage Behan performance.

"Brendan danced the blackbird, sang a medley of bawdy Dublin ballads, told tall tales, played his harmonica, joked and regaled his beholders with a host of very entertaining impressions that included Mussolini, Churchill, Toulouse Lautrec, the babushka-clad old woman of Connemara, Hitler and others," remembered Arthurs. "When Brendan had finished his Hitler impression, he stepped to the centre, snapped his suspenders against his chest, winked and quipped, 'Aye, but there's a thing or two to be said about us aul house painters.'"

The reporters loved it, especially since Behan was delivering this impromptu show, completely sober, while chomping on an enormous cigar. In the article that UPI put out on the wire for the newspapers of America, this was regarded as worth mentioning in the course of an account of his two-hours of singing and raconteuring, a display the reporter regarded as "captivating".

"God made all the Irish happy and all their songs sad," said Behan in between tunes. They jotted it down in their notebook, either not realising or not bothering to report it was a reworking of a classic G.K. Chesterton line.

The journalists accompanied the Behans to the bullfighting ring where Jaime Bravo of Mexico City and Jose Ramon Tirado of Mazatian were top of the bill. If the members of the press were excited at the prospect of what he might get up to in the venue, Beatrice and Arthurs had other concerns on their minds. Brendan had told them he fancied getting into the ring with the bulls. A ludicrous threat but, of course, this was somebody for whom ludicrous carry-on was something of a default setting.

Still, Beatrice couldn't relax during the contests for fear her husband was stupid enough to join in but once he saw the show up close, he was suitably cowed and stayed put. It turned out to be a disappointing spectacle in any case, an "inferior corrida" in which the bulls and the matadors didn't seem too interested in performing for their fans. Eventually, the locals had seen enough. They began jeering and firing the cushions from their seats down into the arena.

"Brendan, now you have seen your first bullfight. What do you think?" asked Don Freedman of the San Diego Tribune.

"It could have been worse," said Behan as the cushions flew past his head. "It could have been folk singing."

The party travelled outside Tijuana too. Arthurs drove them down the coast to the beach resort of Ensenada where Brendan was thrilled to go swimming. The fact he hadn't bothered to pack a swimsuit was, as usual, no impediment to him. That leg of the trip also offered a glimpse into the real Mexico that lay beyond the frontier town glamour and ersatz glitz of Tijuana.

"I loved Mexico," said Beatrice, "though the comparison between the standard of living in Mexico and the United States was tremendous."

Far as her husband had travelled from home, he hadn't

forgotten his pals back in Dublin. On June 12, he picked up a postcard containing work by the artist Diego Rivera and mailed it to his friend John Ryan, former editor of Envoy magazine, in which he mentioned some of his old cronies.

"...Dear Hemingway Ryan,
A strange thing – I was thinking of (Frank) Swift and (Anthony) Cronin and all when I saw this – I shed a tear of tequila into my vaso,
F. Scott Behan.
PS. I'd better say (Patrick) Kavanagh would love this place – I'm quite sure he wouldn't – I hope he's well."

CHAPTER TWELVE

The Leaving Of Los Angeles

You feel like a butterfly in a sausage machine. Behan only stops talking to save breath for singing. I love him because he's the playboy of the western world but you get to feel stultified. You never get a word in edgewise.

ALEXANDER KING, WRITER AND TELEVISION PERSONALITY

LAWRENCE TIERNEY grew up in Brooklyn in the 1920s and 1930s. The son of an Irish policeman, he made his name as an actor playing the notorious crook John Dillinger in the 1945 movie of the same name. Thereafter, he became synonymous with heels in the film noir era, even earning the nickname, "the handsome bad man of the screen". His problem was that he couldn't leave the characters behind and soon earned a reputation for being just as truculent, violent and drunken as the bad guys he played. By the early 1960s, he wasn't working with anything like the regularity of before, studios perhaps put off by his constant brushes with the law.

One day, Tierney knocked at the door of the Behans' apartment at the Montecito. Was he curious to meet a man with a knack for finding trouble that matched his own? Or, was he hopeful that Brendan, with his star in the ascendant around town, might be able to put some work his way? Whatever his motivation, the welcome he received was not warm. Brendan was busy writing when he called and, obviously very happy to see this, Beatrice didn't want her husband disturbed by anybody. Most especially not by a man who was suddenly taking it upon himself to read the most freshly-written lines and to suggest changes.

She phoned Peter Arthurs to come over and help remove the stranger. Presenting himself as Behan's bodyguard, Arthurs asked Tierney to leave because he was interfering with the work being done. There ensued a brief stand-off during which the tough guy eyed up Arthurs, a man with some boxing experience, as Behan sat at his typewriter. No punches were thrown. Tierney eventually departed without any trouble, then phoned back later to invite them all over to a party at his house. When they arrived at chez Tierney that night, he introduced Arthurs and Brendan as a pair of Irish homosexuals.

If that was a suitably bizarre postscript to the incident, the cameo at the Montecito also showed that, despite all the distractions, Behan was, finally, getting some actual work done on "Richard's Cork Leg". A trip to Forest Lawn Memorial Park, the Los Angeles cemetery where a litany of stars had been laid to rest, had fired up his creativity. Arthurs recalled him walking between the headstones that afternoon, searching for the graves of Tyrone Power and Rudolph Valentino, avidly scribbling notes on a guide map of the more famous graves, and, inevitably, being recognised by other tourists on the same trail.

He was so enthused by the sudden flourishing – the increased productivity inevitably coincided with another outbreak of temporary sobriety – that often he'd phone Arthurs at 5 in the morning to read him the best bits from the new material. This interlude where Behan was at work, excited about getting stuff down on paper, and eager to run lines past somebody would be significant for all the wrong reasons. It would turn out to be one of the last times in his life that he applied himself seriously and with any diligence to his craft and managed a sustained bout of writing. A terrible thing to say about somebody two years short of his 40th birthday.

They must have cut a funny trio around town, the drunken

Irish playwright, his long-suffering wife, and their handsome younger friend. Certainly, it was a curious arrangement. Aside from the fact he was having an affair or at the very least ongoing sexual encounters with Brendan, which may or may not have been known to Beatrice, Arthurs spent so much time with the couple he got an up-close glimpse of their relationship. And some of what he saw wasn't pretty. He claims that he witnessed Brendan hitting Beatrice several times.

"Then in a full fiery orbit, he was up and lashing out with a volley of lightning quick, short left hooks and right upper cuts that sent her flying up against the stove," wrote Arthurs of an assault prompted by Beatrice forgetting to bring milk back to the short-stay apartment they'd moved into on Franklin Avenue, north of Hollywood Boulevard. "She shrieked in horror as Brendan kicked her. I grabbed hold of him, put my left arm around his throat, and forced his chin upwards. He grimaced in pain. Beatrice pulled herself together, got up off the floor and grabbed hold of my wrist, 'No, no, no, don't hurt Brendan...'"

There were other incidents, all recounted in gruesome and convincing detail by Arthurs in his memoir. Most culminated in him intervening on Beatrice's behalf and then, in the classic way of the abusive relationship, her beseeching him not to visit retribution on her husband.

"The reality, however – and this is a view shared by many who knew them after 1960 – is that she was regularly at the receiving end of his violent rage," wrote Michael O'Sullivan. "Again, she bore it because she knew she was dealing with an extremely sick man."

Nobody else was privy to this side of Behan's character and in Hollywood, the invitations came thick and fast to the hotel. Much like New York, Los Angeles was a town where everybody was eager to rub shoulders with the latest headline-grabber. Ernie Kovacs, a man now regarded as one of the most innovative and influential television comedians ever, asked them along to a typically star-studded party at his house, with Shirley MacLaine, Kim Novak and Jack Lemmon among the guest list. Not even that trio however could compete with the wattage of one particular celebrity that night.

"I met Elizabeth Taylor," said Beatrice years later. "She is very beautiful. She and Brendan talked and talked about hospitals. She had been in the London Clinic and he had been in hospital in Canada."

When it came time for the Behans to leave town (Beatrice was, as usual, a lot more eager to depart than her husband), Brendan had been on the dry for more than two weeks. He'd been in Hollywood just over a month yet his departure was still news enough to make the bulging gossip columns of the newspapers, right below the latest speculation about the turbulent marriage of Robert Wagner and Natalie Wood. The strange circumstances of Behan's leave-taking must have been what caught the editors' eyes; he threw himself a going-away party before catching a train back to New York.

On Tuesday, June 20, he invited a dozen or so of his closest friends in the city to enjoy some farewell drinks in the main dining room at Union Station. Arthurs drove the Behans there, getting pulled over by a motorcycle cop on the way. As the officer came to the window, Arthurs flashed the business card of Kenneth Vils, a ranking officer of the Los Angeles Police Department, and somebody who'd befriended the Behans over the course of their stay. The policeman saw the name, and, instead of issuing a ticket, he offered to escort them the rest of the way.

When the press saw the uniformed cop and Vils both present at the shindig, they reported that the officers were there to make sure that Behan got on the train and left town for good. Definitely a case of not letting the facts get in the way of a good story and possibly what the readers would have expected given his previous hell-raising around town. The truth is Behan was on his best behaviour, buying drinks all round but sticking to the soda water and the coffee himself, and boasting that his burst of writing ensured "Richard's Cork Leg" was almost finished.

"It's about sex, politics and religion, in that order, in a ratio of about 60-20-20," he said.

Among those present were Arthur Shields (an Irish-born actor, a veteran of the Easter Rising and younger brother of Barry Fitzgerald), and director Michael O'Herlihy (a Dubliner making his way in Hollywood where he would go on to do episodes of everything from "Maverick" in one era to "The A-Team" in another). The press lapped it up as Behan called Hollywood "a good place to hide out in" and regaled them with stories about his various negotiations with movie moguls and cops.

"I met some humorous and intellectual policemen," he said, "and I had to meet a stern judge later."

His form was ebullient because real progress had been made on "Richard's Cork Leg". It was nowhere near finished and never quite would be but, freshly infused with a range of American influences, ranging from Forest Lawn to the Harlem Globetrotters, there was much more of the play there than before. Certainly, there was enough of a manuscript for it to be used as a prop in a dramatic going-away scene concocted on the station platform to give the television crew who'd turned up something to work with for the evening news.

When the Behans boarded the train (ironically named Placid Waters), the cameras filmed their departure, staying on them even as they made their way to their seats. As the engines finally started to chug, Brendan stood up, suddenly pretending to realise he'd forgotten the manuscript for the play. He started shouting and gesticulating at Beatrice and after plenty of hamming it up, the cameras cut to Arthurs who just remembered (for their benefit) that he had been given the pages for safe-keeping.

At this point, the train was starting to move so Arthurs began running along the platform until he reached their carriage. Then Brendan, with Beatrice in true comic-caper fashion holding on to his legs lest he fall, leaned out the window to grab the play in the nick of time, being sure to mug for the cameras once he did. Yet one more hilarious cameo of the notoriety he enjoyed. That so many fast friends and acquaintances had turned up to bid him adieu was one thing. That a television news crew was on hand, as well as a gaggle of press reporters and photographers, was something else altogether.

Barely five weeks after arriving in a city that boasted more famous and wannabe famous people than any other place on earth, his decision to leave and the manner of his departure was newsworthy. Whatever else could be said, he had, as usual, left his mark.

"During Brendan's round of taverns, one gentleman got whacked in the mouth, and another hapless fellow received a bloody nose," wrote Joe Finnigan for UPI. "Who threw the punches that landed on those surprised faces is still a matter of discrete discussion in movie circles. But Brendan is known to have been in the immediate vicinity when one punch was thrown. The colourful author was often the subject of talk in a Hollywood that no longer has the corner on individuality and zany antics. In fact, some old-timers said Behan had given Hollywood the colour it's been sorely lacking of late."

The four-day train journey back to New York, was remarkably free of incident.

"Do you know I had twenty-six pieces of luggage on the way home?" said Beatrice. "I don't really know where all the stuff came from – though a lot of them held books that Brendan bought, and books are never portable. I had to pay excess baggage at every railway station on the way back."

His return to his old stomping ground however immediately encountered obstacles. At the Algonquin Hotel, Andrew Anspach (the manager) told the Behans there was no longer room at the inn. Having spent much of the previous four months reading about Brendan's violent, drunken brushes with the law, from Toronto to Los Angeles, Anspach decided their reservation counted for naught. He couldn't risk the good name of his establishment on a guest capable of doing just about anything once he had drink taken.

"Drinking wasn't part of our deal, Brendan," said Anspach. "You promised you'd stay on the wagon and you haven't done so. I can't take you back into the hotel."

Anspach had been a good friend when they first arrived in the city. He'd accompanied the couple to literary and showbiz parties, and as part of the hotel's concierge service, arranged for the front desk to give Brendan cash as he needed it. Which, of course, was often. Now this man stood in front of them in the lobby of the most storied literary hotel in the city and told them they'd have to go elsewhere. It was such a shock Brendan seemed bemused by the news. How could an establishment that welcomed him with such open arms now shut its doors in his face? If he was perplexed, Beatrice was just sad.

"I related the Algonquin to those first happy months in New York. I remembered the pleasure it gave him to sit with other writers at the Round Table. I remembered heads turning whenever he was paged. And I remembered how his skin glowed from the shower on that first evening in our suite when the whiskey bottles for his relatives lay unopened on the table."

Not even a year had passed since he'd first arrived at the Algonquin but the drinking and carousing of the previous months had taken their toll, not just on his public image but his physical well-being. He was a long way removed now from the somewhat healthy character who stepped off the plane at Idlewild in September, 1960 evincing the obvious benefits of months of prolonged sobriety. By this time he was increasingly suffering the side effects from the abuse of alcohol and was cutting a more pathetic figure too.

The rejection by Anspach hit him so hard that when he and Beatrice walked past the hotel later that summer, he wanted to sneak in to have a look around the lobby to see who was there. Once, the porters at the Algonquin found him waiting for the elevator. He'd wandered in and apparently forgot he was no longer staying there. A cameo of forgetfulness or the pitiful act of somebody struggling to believe the place which tolerated the excesses of so many other writers through the decades had declared him persona non grata? Probably a bit of both.

It is pointed that when Behan wrote a letter to President John F. Kennedy on July 15th, he still gave the Algonquin as his address.

A Divine Vasal (sic),

I would not be so presumptuous to comment on matters appertaining to the relationship between presidents and prelates but I think the following anecdote about the 15th century head of your maternal clan might interest you from a genealogical point of view. Mac (check spelling) Iarla Fitzgerald, Earl of Kildare, poet, soldier, known as the Mac Gearailt Mor, or the great Fitzgerald, was summoned to Rome to explain his conduct in burning the cathedral. The pope asked why he had committed this great sacrilege. His Lordship replied: I declare to Jesus your holiness, I would never have done it but I thought the archbishop was inside. I saw you speak on 7th Avenue and a man said to me – 'even Menken (sic) would have voted for him!'

In New York and indeed, in America, 1961 was the summer of Roger Maris and Mickey Mantle, a pair of New York Yankees locked in a battle to chase down Babe Ruth's record for most home runs hit in a single baseball season. At a time when baseball was still the national obsession, very few people were as famous as Mantle and Maris. One particular morning, Americans reading Earl Wilson's nationally syndicated gossip column from New York learned about Mantle eating steaks at Danny's restaurant and then about Behan wearing a souvenir "Hug Me, Kiss Me" hat to dinner at The Crystal Room. This is the level of celebrity he had achieved.

One gossip maven mentioned him being spotted singing "Mack the Knife" at Versailles in Greenwich Village, that nugget appearing in between reports about Jimmy Hoffa and Marlene Dietrich. The company he kept. Another story ran about him accompanying the band at Luchow's where the manager Jan Mitchell told the band not to play anything he couldn't sing.

No matter what he did, however mundane, it made it into the papers.

He shook hands with Dr. A.B. Webstein to have his missing teeth replaced, with just one proviso, he had to promise to sit still long enough for the dentist to work. Following successful meetings in Hollywood, and in order to prepare for future endeavours, he claimed he'd been teaching himself to write screenplays by using the script from "Hiroshima Mon Amour", a movie he'd seen in Los Angeles with Arthurs a few weeks earlier. At an event in the Metropole Hotel, he wouldn't pose for a press photograph until his beer was replaced by a glass of milk. A newsworthy moment!

Beatrice figured as a bit-part player in some of the reports too. Behan was having lunch at the Monte Rosa when she walked in just as he was in mid-song. She leaned over to kiss him and Behan announced to the restaurant, "It's love." After pausing for comic effect, he continued, "Also, she wants to smell my breath to make sure I haven't been drinking." In another column brief, Leonard Lyons recounted how, in the middle of a long diatribe to an audience in a restaurant, Brendan pointed to his wife and said, "She doesn't talk much." She gave him a look and replied, "How would you know? You've never given me a chance to say a word!"

None of the New York papers thought it newsworthy that Behan went to the Polo Grounds on June 26th. He was there to see a Shamrock Rovers selection draw 2-2 with Petah Tikva from Israel in the International Soccer League, a short-lived summer competition run over several weeks in the US. But he enjoyed the excursion enough to mention it in a letter he wrote to Liam Creagh, a friend back in Ireland. In the same missive, he described Hollywood as "...not much of a place – like Foxrock multiplied by a hundred – but my sort of people and bags of money lying round for a hard-working boy like me."

He might still have had star power and there's no doubt Hollywood had work for him if he was able but, in reality, Behan's circumstances had changed. For the first time in years, money was getting tight. So tight in fact that Beatrice had booked their passage home on the Holland American liner, the Statendem. As the clocked ticked down towards their departure, he could be found more and more across the river in Hoboken, frequenting bars like the Clam Broth, a place popular with the New Jersey dockworkers, drawn by the prospect of free chowder, a rule barring women from the premises, and a 5am opening.

Hoboken was where he ended up after a binge that began at Jim Downey's on July 26th when he told reporters he was celebrating "the summer festival". He did not seem in such a festive mood when he was found wandering aimlessly outside the Municipal Building in Hoboken near dawn the next morning.

Dan Kiely, a local cop who knew him from previous encounters, discovered Behan shoeless and clueless. He took him to the station, put him in a cell to sleep it off and phoned Beatrice.

The Statendem would sail without the Behans on board. Brendan was on his way to the New Jersey Medical Centre for treatment. It was either that or charges would have to be pressed. They drove to the hospital in Kiely's car and it was then that the reality of their new financial situation hit Beatrice. She didn't have the money to stump up for another hotel so she had to ask Brendan's cousin Paul Bourke, who lived in New Jersey with his wife Catherine, to help her out. The Bourkes gave her one of their children's bedrooms for as long as she needed it.

Although the press got wind of the story, the police described him as "under the weather" but not drunk. And Dr. John Mackin, the physician in charge of his case, told reporters he would need a week in hospital to recover. He didn't need that. Within days, he was discharged and, while waiting for the next boat home, it was decided to keep him away from New York with its all too obvious temptations. Instead, Joseph Brill, a celebrity lawyer who'd defended Norman Mailer on charges he'd stabbed his wife, drove Behan to the small town of Margaretville in the Catskill Mountains of upstate New York.

Brill had a holiday home in the area but he booked his guest into The Kass Inn. There, the lawyer told the staff to keep quiet about the celebrity who had come to rest and recuperate after recent travails. They left him alone, and, perhaps more surprisingly, Behan left them alone too. When Al Farber arrived to work a shift in the bar one afternoon, he discovered Behan sitting there on his own. Not drunk. Not quarrelsome. They chatted for a while but it was impossible to reconcile this quiet man passing the time of day with the hell-raiser of tabloid legend.

Of course, Brill's request for privacy was honoured by everybody except Behan himself. Even on his best behaviour, he had to get out and socialise. He wandered around the town, loitering in the drug store and the barber shop, enjoying and, no doubt, dominating the conversations. He bought himself a bathing suit in another outlet and confessed that Margaretville was much different from how he imagined small American towns to be, having seen so many of them in the movies.

"The people of Margaretville are friendly," he said in a brief interview with the Catskill Mountain News that made short work of Brill attempting to hide him away. "They don't ask you how it feels to be a famous person, but want to know how you are, how your family is doing, and how you like the Catskills and the everyday things."

Far from the madding crowd, Behan saw a different side of American life. On Sunday afternoon, he climbed into Joseph Brill's jeep for a tour of the area. At one point, they drove to the top of the Plattekill Mountain Ski Resort which had opened just three years earlier. There, Behan got out and went into the observation tower to take in the valley below. On the trip back through the forest, he saw more of the land than he might have hoped for. The jeep got mired in mud and it took himself, Brill and Brill's son Walter four hours of pulling and dragging to extricate the vehicle before they could resume their journey.

On Tuesday, August 1st, the Behans caught the 9am bus out of Margaretville and travelled the three hours back to New York city. The next day, they boarded the Queen Mary and headed for home.

Upon arriving back in Dublin, Behan announced he would be returning to California in October to finish two screenplays, one of which was about the Easter Rising, neither of which would ever see the light of day. Walter Winchell reported this detail in his syndicated column in American newspapers, along with a quote from Behan saying, "The one thing you miss over there is the fresh air over here!" Winchell couldn't resist adding his own rejoinder, "Especially when you stay bagged, plastered, fried, crocked, woofied and squifft!"

That wasn't the only bizarre postscript to this particular trip.

"When I came home to Dublin, I found a letter which contained the understatement of the year," said Behan. "It began 'Dear Mr. Behan, you will be surprised to hear from me...'"

The author was Reverend Billy Graham. Unfortunately, that's as much of the communication from America's leading preacher that Behan ever divulged.

CHAPTER THIRTEEN

Father Doesn't Know Best

There is nothing I would rather do than write – except talk in pubs, restaurants, bistros, saloons. However you get no $ or £ for that.

BRENDAN BEHAN, ESQUIRE MAGAZINE, FEBRUARY, 1962

IN the months after her dalliance with Behan at the Mark Hopkins hotel in San Francisco, Valerie Danby-Smith became involved in helping Ernest Hemingway's wife with the handling of her husband's estate following his suicide on July 2nd, 1961. She was busy enough to try to ignore the growing signs her body was sending her that she was pregnant with the child of a crazed Irish alcoholic. By year's end, however, she was back in New York and facing up to the reality of her physical condition and the responsibilities she now had.

Her initial instinct was to say nothing and rear the child on her own but others counselled differently. When she told her friends in Manhattan, a few of whom were also friends of Behan's, some urged her to tell him about the impending arrival. Many hoped that fatherhood might be the landmark event that would finally cause him to swear off the bottle. A couple just advised that informing him was the right thing to do. In the end, Danby-Smith picked up the phone in early January, 1962 and called Dublin.

"The moment I broke the news to Brendan he was elated," wrote Danby-Smith. "'I'm coming over,' he said without hesitation. 'I'll be there as soon as I can.' Over the next few days, he telephoned me a dozen times. He said he had talked to Beatrice, and if I would agree, they wanted to bring up the child together in Ireland. Surely I could see this was the best thing. After grave thought and consideration, I gave him the answer he wanted. It seemed that might be the only the way this strange quadrangle could work out in everyone's best interests."

Whether or not he had even talked to his wife about the chances of them rearing the child together (Beatrice never publicly admitted as much), he had resolved, for one reason or another, to go to America.

"I have recovered from my usual illness, too much barley juice," wrote Behan in mid-January in a letter to Leonard Lyons. "I am off it now. America was very good for me. Here, there is nothing to do but drink, which is one good reason I'd like to get back to the States. I am interested in working out a play with American actors. If there is another tour of the 'The Hostage', I shall go over and accompany the show."

As chance would have it, Perry Bruskin, stage manager of the production of "The Hostage" at the Cort Theatre back in 1960, was now helming an off-Broadway revival of the play that was due to open on February 5th, 1962. Three days before opening night, Behan left for New York. As is so often the case with him, there are different accounts about the manner of his departure.

In the most popular version, he told Beatrice he was heading out to Cole's to meet a friend for a pint and simply never returned, leaving her waiting at the dinner table for his return. In another, he left the house to buy a packet of cigarettes and ended up catching a taxi to Shannon Airport. In her memoir, his wife claimed she simply decided not to go with him. Whatever the exact circumstances of his leaving, he ended up in Shannon and on a flight to Idlewild.

That same weekend, Peter Arthurs, back at work as a merchant seaman since his adventure with the Behans in Hollywood the previous summer, was onboard the SS Bents Fort which docked at Petty's Island, Philadelphia with a cargo of black sulphur. A union representative boarded the ship to inform Arthurs a Mr. Behan had been on to the SIU offices, trying to track down his whereabouts. Arthurs called the Algonquin Hotel, presuming that's where he'd be, but the staff informed him Behan was no longer welcome there. They gave him the number of The Bristol on 48th Street.

When he finally got through to the new, much less salubrious and distinguished lodgings, Behan sounded distraught and urged him to hightail it to New York where he had some urgent matters (his impending fatherhood, amongst them) to discuss. Arthurs told the captain of the ship his father had passed away in Ireland, securing his early release from the vessel. Within hours, he was at The Bristol, where he found his old friend/worst enemy in between sessions and in a state of some disrepair.

When Arthurs opened the door to Behan's room, he was sitting naked with the New York Times opened on the floor in front of him, devouring a mountain of Chinese food that he'd placed upon the paper, stopping occasionally to swig from a fast-emptying bottle of Jack Daniels.

"A very distraught-looking man dressed in a bellhop's uniform stood against the wall with his hands in his pockets," wrote Arthurs. 'Excuse me, Sir,' he said. 'My name is Davies. I'm the head bellhop here. Do you know Mr. Behan personally?'...The bellman pushed a piece of paper into my hand, and said, 'Here, will you get this money from him? He refuses to pay me. If I don't collect, I'm out six dollars and 85 cents.'"

When Arthurs asked Behan why he was unwilling to pay for the food he ordered, he was too busy stuffing his face with ribs and egg rolls to respond. Eventually, Arthurs found Behan's jacket, and took a five pound note that was tucked into his passport, handed it to Davies and assured him this would cover the bill and compensate him for the extra hassle. Crisis averted, he then listened to Behan outline the story of the unplanned pregnancy and all the attendant drama coming with it.

Next morning, the pair of them went to visit the heavily pregnant Valerie Danby-Smith at the Hemingways' apartment on 62nd Street where she was staying. As the two people closest to him at that point in that city, the future mother of his child and his constant companion/sometime lover didn't exactly hit it off. Indeed, Arthurs claimed it was very obvious Danby-Smith had nothing but disdain for him. As per usual, Behan appeared unaffected by the tension bothering those in his orbit and in any case, the baby was almost due.

Behan was in his room at The Bristol on February 12th, 1962 when he received the phone call telling him baby Brendan had been born. He was reportedly thrilled with the news. That he was the father appeared to have been well-known around the city. Indeed, there are reports that whispers of the impending arrival had been doing the rounds for weeks if not months, and he may have blurted it out once or twice himself during drunken soliloquies. That it never appeared in print anywhere was perhaps down to this being a different era of morality in journalism, not to mention that the gossip columnists, principally Lyons, seemed to have a genuine fondness for Behan. They may have been trying to protect him and/or keep his show on the road a little longer.

"Soon after I came home from the hospital with baby Brendan, we had a grand baptism party with Lar and Helen Dunne (her friends who lived in Great Neck, Long Island)," wrote Danby-Smith. "Now Brendan broke it to me gently: Beatrice had changed her mind. In fact, once she had had a chance to think about what had happened, she was very angry. However, Brendan said consolingly, he had talked to his mother.

She was thrilled at having another grandson and would willingly bring him up on her own."

Again, none of the above was ever confirmed by Beatrice, but it didn't really matter because Danby-Smith wasn't buying this option. Kathleen, famously, the mother of all the Behans, was a formidable character (Smith actually describes the matriarch in her own book as "magnificent"). However, the mother of the new-born thought Dublin and a grandmother already well into her 70s was not the environment in which she imagined her baby growing up. She decided to keep the child and Behan vouchsafed he would provide for them both. If he was drawing down the kind of money then to allow him make such bold assurances, he was also leading a lifestyle that wasn't cut out for parental responsibility.

Three days before Danby-Smith gave birth, Brendan had celebrated his 39th birthday at Monte Rosa on 48th Street, one of his favourite haunts in the city. "It is an Italian restaurant, with Spanish waiters, a Jewish proprietor and a largely Irish clientele, and is one of the most interesting places I was ever in my life," he once wrote. "It is also a bit of a madhouse, but that's beside the point."

On the night of these festivities, he ensured it lived up to the last part of that billing. Whether it was the milestone of a birthday or the knowledge he had an estranged wife in Dublin and a pregnant woman in New York, Behan was in foul humour. To cheer him up, Viola Lipsett, wife of the owner Jack, presented him with a Delft teapot with the words "Brendan Behan his teapot" inscribed on it. She also gave him a copy of the New York Daily News from October 27th, 1960 when he'd made the cover after marching on stage at the Cort Theatre the previous night, shouting "You're making a muck of me play!"

A wonderful gesture. Or not. Depending on what mood he was in.

"Brendan sighed with boredom," wrote Arthurs, "then with a quick violent smash of the hand, he sent the teapot and the newspaper flying. 'Oh Brendan, how could you do such a terrible thing?' Viola lamented, gathering up the teapot. Brendan reached down, picked up the paper, tore it into shreds and sent it flying about in a hail of confetti."

Essentially, he appears to have spent much of the week surrounding the birth on the lash. As a man with so much money invested in his writing, the publisher Bernard Geis was alarmed enough at reports of Behan's carousing to charge his publicist Letty Cottin Pogrebin with a simple task: "Find Brendan and see if you can get him working." A smart young woman who knew exactly what she was dealing with, Pogrebin began the search by phoning police precincts and bars. The only information she gleaned from the initial ring-round was confirmation that Behan was blazing a trail through the city.

In the absence of a definite lead, she decided to lure the big fish in with some bait. She began to visit his favoured haunts, a long and ever-growing list, and at each stop, told the bartenders and the barflies to pass on a piece of paper with an address and the following message to Behan; "Meet Letty at a midnight to dawn party in Greenwich Village tonight." Her thinking was that an all-night party would surely be enough to draw him in. So it proved. At 3am, she spotted the tousle-haired figure arriving at the shindig in familiar style. With a rope keeping his trousers up and no socks under his shoes, the Dublin accent was soon at full-throttle, offering up a song, a bawdy folk number from World War II, for the crowd.

..We've tried it once or twice

And found it rather nice

Roll me over lay me down and do it again

Roll me over in the clover, roll me over lay me down and do it again

Pogrebin had got her man. He was three sheets to the wind but at least he was in sight. She introduced herself and came clean about the fact she'd used a friend's party to locate him. She even admitted she was trying to get him back on the wagon so he might start writing again. Not a preposterous suggestion given that he owed Geis an advance well into five figures. Before the conversation could go any farther, Behan was spirited away and soon surrounded by a legion of adoring literary types, thrilled to be getting the full-on drunken Irish writer experience.

Eventually, Pogrebin got him away from the crowd, bundled him into a cab and brought him back to the Bristol, by which time he was assuring her he'd be ready to write first thing the next day. All was going well until Pogrebin made to leave the lobby. Showing the ability to turn dark in an instant, Behan picked up a heavy ashtray and assured her he'd smash the front window of the place if she didn't come up to his room. Inebriated as he was, and to that point in her life, she claimed to have never seen anybody drunker, Behan threatened to cause a scene and to give the publicist all the newspaper headlines she could handle.

Deciding to avoid a fracas, she walked him to the elevator, grabbing his arm and calming him down. Once they reached his room however, Behan flipped again.

"He grabbed my shoulders, threw me on the bed and dived on top of me," wrote Pogrebin. "If I had pause for any thought at all – other than shock and fear – it was that someone so totally soused could still have such strength and energy. I kicked and squirmed and pummelled him. He was beyond reason. My protests were getting futile. My struggling was getting me nowhere. I didn't scream for fear that my saviours – given the fact of this unsavoury hotel – might be worse than my attacker.

"In full face of the terror that I might actually be raped, I uttered a plea from the primordial depths within me: 'Please Brendan, don't! I'm a nice Jewish girl.' Those words somehow hit him like a cold shower. He bolted upright. He sat primly on the edge of the bed and with one hand stroking my cheek, he said: 'Well for Jaysus sake, why didn't you say that in the first place?' While I cringed and trembled in one corner of the room, Brendan paced the floor, suddenly sober and very intense."

Now filled with remorse, Behan began expounding on his theories about the similarities between the Irish and the Jews, and their mutual sufferings and oppressions. Eventually, in a bizarre sequel to a frightening episode that showcased the darkest corner of his sexual psyche, Behan walked Pogrebin back downstairs, and waited with her on the street as she hailed a cab for home just after dawn. Perhaps even more bizarrely, the pair continued to maintain a working professional relationship, starting when Behan showed up at the Geis's office next morning to work on the manuscript for "Confessions of an Irish Rebel", the proposed sequel to "Borstal Boy".

In this state of advanced disrepair, Behan was still box office enough to be garnering invitations to media events and demands to appear on television shows, On Tuesday, February 13th, he was scheduled to be on the Jack Paar show with Joey Bishop, a member of the fabled Rat Pack, Peggy Cass, an Academy Award winning actress, and The Smothers Brothers, an up and coming comedy act who were darlings of the counter-culture.

That he was regarded as a perfect fit for this kind of line-up showed that, despite the chaos and tumult in his private and professional life, Behan's star still glittered. Well, it could glitter if it received some spit and polish on occasion. With this in mind, Pogrebin arrived at the hotel that evening with the expressed instruction to make him over so he'd be ready for prime time. Never an easy task with somebody who often slept in his clothes, it was made even more difficult by the fact he'd flown to New York on this occasion with just the clothes he stood up in.

In typical style, he wasn't there when she arrived anyway. A homeless man outside the hotel told her Behan was at the bar in the Silver Rail on 7th Avenue and 23rd Street in Greenwich Village. A popular hang-out for prostitutes, pimps and drug-dealers, the Silver Rail was run by a legendary 300lb African-American lesbian. Inevitably, it became one of his favourite bars in the city. When Pogrebin got there, she found him crumpled in a heap beneath a table, sawdust speckling his clothes and hair. Where else would he have been on the day when he was wetting the baby's head?

"Letty me love," said Behan as she roused him from his slumber, "what in St. Peter's name are you doing down here on the barroom floor?"

An attempted clean-up in the bathroom of the Silver Rail only underlined what a state of disrepair his wardrobe was in. It was nearly nine at night, way beyond closing time for most stores. Pogrebin, showing the resourcefulness that would lead her to found MS magazine with Gloria Steinem years later, consulted her Diner's Club directory and found two stores uptown that kept late hours.

"Cy Martin's was one of the most elegant haberdashery stores on Broadway," wrote Arthurs. "Its window was aglow with autographed photos of famous baseball players and movie stars. Brendan eyed the pictures disdainfully. Inside the store, Brendan quickly disrobed and charged around in the raw, cursing and knocking over racks of expensive clothing, then he reenacted the Glasnevin shoot-out, improvising the gun with a shoe tree. The bespectacled salesman pulled the curtains, doused the lights, asked a few female customers to leave, then locked the doors. 'Please tell Mr. Behan to at least put on his shorts,' the man pleaded, while he wheedled, and coaxed Brendan to dress."

Two complete outfits were purchased, along with a belt to replace the cord that was keeping his trousers around his waist. He conceded to putting on socks, refused to allow them buy him new shoes and then got into an argument about an attempt to purchase him some fresh underwear.

"Me and Marilyn Monroe, we never wear the stuff," said the man who later that night would be appearing on television screens all across America, living up to his reputation as the outrageous and witty Irish playwright. Nobody watching was any wiser to the fact he'd been paralytic under a table in a dive bar a matter of hours earlier.

"When I heard from friends it was an unhappy visit, I wrote to Perry (Bruskin) and begged him to send Brendan home to me," wrote Beatrice Behan. "I feared he might die in New York, and Perry understood. It was a city with no room for a drunken playwright. I imagined Brendan lying in his apartment, unable to call for help, wanting me beside him."

His wife's fears that he might die in New York were well-founded given the way he was carousing, but her assessment of the lonely drunk locked away in a room was wide of the mark. He remained a popular figure and an endless source of fascination. William Shawn, editor of the New Yorker, had commissioned Brendan Gill, one of its writers, to do a profile of Behan for the pre-eminent literary magazine in America. The article was never written but the two men became good friends, at least for a while.

Gill would take Behan to The Coffee House, a private club on West Forty-Fifth Street where the Dubliner's lack of teeth proved problematic when confronted with the establishment's legendary steaks. Once, he arrived into the place with a copy of the Finnish edition of "The Borstal Boy", the writer in him boyishly thrilled to see his work translated into a language he'd never heard spoken. Until that night. One of the waitresses happened to be from Finland and she sat down with Behan and Gill by an open fire and read him extracts from his work.

The unlikely duo also dined regularly at Schraft's, a more down-home restaurant in Times Square. There, Gill would watch as Behan skimmed through the day's newspapers to see if he was mentioned in any of the gossip columns or theatre notices. There was no question this attention was like oxygen to him at all times. Much as he complained about fame, he seemed to have an endless appetite for his own infamy. And, Gill witnessed both the harmless and the offensive side of that tendency. More than once, he saw Behan grope or attempt to grope the Irish waitresses who worked in Schraft's. Every grab and lunge came freighted with some sexual comment or innuendo, and, perhaps typically of the tolerance of this kind of behaviour in that era, none of the women ever reported him.

Against that background it's perhaps as well for Behan that Gill never got around to writing the piece for the magazine. That said, the journalist was fond enough of his subject to bring him into his own home, replete with the new branch of his family.

"On one occasion, [Valerie] and Brendan brought their winsome infant out to the Gills' house in Bronxville, where a snapshot was taken of four Brendans in a row; two Brendan Behans, my eldest grandchild Brendan Larson, and me," wrote Brendan Gill. "A superb actor, Brendan entertained us throughout the afternoon with imitations, my favourite was his imitation of a pious adolescent boy advancing to the communion rail, accepting the unleavened wafer – by then nothing less than the body of God – on his tongue, and returning down the aisle with hands reverently clasped and with his tongue feverishly working away to get God down off the roof of his mouth and duly swallowed."

The challenge of being a new father was counterbalanced by days and nights spent on the skite with Arthurs. The one sop to good living and health was his love of swimming, a passion that often took the pair of them across the river to Brooklyn Heights where the St. George Hotel, then the largest in the city, boasted the biggest indoor saltwater pool in the world in its basement. It was quite the facility with three diving boards at the deep end, a waterfall at the shallow end, and plenty to appeal to an overgrown child fond of splashing about and prone to losing his shorts when performing acrobatic stunts.

According to Arthurs, there was something else that attracted Behan to the place. In that time, the St. George, with its steam rooms, saunas, and enormous locker-room full of nooks and crannies was a popular gay haunt.

"Another gaggle of daily patrons who flocked to the pool were the taut-muscled coffee-coloured, clean-limbed Hispanic youths of New York," wrote Arthurs in his memoir. "Many of these broad-minded ethnics allowed the older homosexuals to fondle them for a fee. For these teenage boys, this was an easy way to earn a few extra dollars. Brendan took advantage of this situation. These were the specific type of clear-complected youths who sent his eyes aflutter. On a number of occasions when Brendan had suddenly disappeared for a considerable period of time, I would eventually come upon him sitting on one of the long wooden benches in the locker room, or in a kneeling position behind one of the supporting columns in the basketball court, sucking the cock and caressing the buttocks of a well-constructed teenager."

Inevitably, a man leading as promiscuous a lifestyle as this started to suffer the consequences. Following his attempted rape of her, Letty Cottin Pogrebin's view of him changed. She regarded him as less of a charming eccentric and more somebody with a mental illness.

"Berney Geis asked me to take Brendan to a psychiatrist, Robert Naiman, to see if therapy could save him from his alcoholism," said Pogrebin. "While we were talking to Dr. Naiman, Brendan asked if he was a real doctor. The psychiatrist said you have to be a physician to be a psychiatrist, at which point, Brendan dropped his pants and asked if Dr. Naiman could diagnose whatever was troubling his private parts. Dr. Naiman immediately said it was 'the clap.'"

CHAPTER FOURTEEN

The Village Idiot

Greenwich Village has to me, since the age of 14, been the
Killarney of America, and you have made me proud and happy

BRENDAN BEHAN, LETTER TO THE VILLAGE VOICE, FEBRUARY, 1959.

PERRY BRUSKIN'S revival of "The Hostage" was showing at One Sheridan Square in Greenwich Village. A typical off-Broadway theatre space, it was located underneath an Italian restaurant in one of the hippest parts of New York city. Patrons who paid $4.50 for tickets were warned to beware the 17 treacherous steps leading down to a lobby that contained a tiny coat check, a ticket office and a ladies' bathroom. In a bizarre feature, it also had a currency exchange window, introduced because so many foreigners began turning up to the box office. Most major currencies were accepted and one of the newspapers ran a story about this development under the headline: "How many shekels?"

While the crowd filed in and made their way along the eight rows of seats placed around the three stone pillars that were keeping the tiny house upright, "Molly Malone" played over the PA. The stage was a wooden platform raised just six inches off the stone floor and the spectators at the front were near enough to reach out and touch the actors. The intimacy of the situation added greatly to the spectacle. In the playbill for the show, Behan had a paragraph that became one of his more famous credos, and reminded everybody that even as his writing was being derailed by his lifestyle, there was so much talent there.

"I respect kindness to human beings," he wrote, "first of all, and kindness to animals. I don't respect the law; I have a total irreverence for anything connected with society except that which makes the roads safer, the beer stronger and the food cheaper, and the old men and old women warmer in the winter and happier in the summer."

The play had been substantially revamped and worked over since its stint on Broadway. Many playwrights would have been perturbed by this type of tinkering with their text. Not this one. "I'm not too upset about it," said Behan. "After all, it's not as if I've written fucking Genesis." Some might argue the changes were for the better. This version of the play was described by the New York Times as "irreverent, mad and mirth-provoking" and ended up running for 545 performances, a statistic that spoke to the quality of the play and the production.

Not that it was to everybody's liking.

"The play was shocking," wrote Jim Bishop, a nationally-syndicated columnist who also mentioned in his review that the ticket taker the night he visited was a Negro with a Van Dyke beard. "The audience took the vulgarity to its heart. It roared approval and laughed and slapped its thighs....the plot is both cynical and pointless...It is possible that he is a playwright. If so, I have missed the point, exactly as I have missed the point in all of Tennessee Williams' plays. Still the tiny cellar theatre was jammed. At intermission time, the people pressed forward to the exit to smoke a cigarette and talk learnedly of the 'message' they heard in the play."

It was perhaps just as well Bishop went on a night when Behan himself wasn't present because of course, that type of cameo gave any evening an entirely different tone. As some found out to their cost.

Carla Rotolo handled the lights for the production and her younger sister Suze was working the concession stand that opened before the play and during the intermission. At the time,

18 year old Suze was dating a young folk singer called Bob Dylan who'd moved to New York from Minnesota just a year earlier. The couple were living together in an apartment at 161 West Fourth Street, just around the corner from the theatre, and the pair of them were immersed in the music, arts and protest politics of Greenwich Village at that time.

"I was standing in the back of the theatre watching the play one evening when Behan himself wandered in," wrote Rotolo. "If Behan happened to be in the city where one of his plays was being put on, he had a habit of showing up and joining the performance. It made for interesting theatre at times, especially when he engaged the actors in some improvisation. But he was a bit of a drinker and could completely disrupt the play if he was in his cups. I ran to the phone and called Bobby at home to tell him Brendan Behan was at the theatre and he should come by."

Dylan was 20 years old that night and weeks away from releasing his first album. He already had a minor reputation in the folk scene around the city but there was no hint yet he had the talent and the wherewithal to become an icon for the ages. Back at the apartment, the young singer knew enough of Behan's writing and reputation to jump up and run down the street, excited by the opportunity to see the man, the legend, live and in living colour. And he was certainly all of those three that evening.

"Behan was very drunk," wrote Rotolo. "Listing left and right, he wandered onto the stage, and waving his hands about, made an incoherent speech to the actors. Then he abruptly teetered off the stage and out the door. He staggered up the stairs of the theatre with Bob right behind him. Bob followed him to The White Horse, hoping for a conversation, but Behan was in no shape for anything remotely resembling talk and eventually passed out."

The tableau painted by Rotolo is equal parts sad and revealing. Here was Behan being pursued along Hudson Street by a young fan who was trying to find a voice for his own talent, a young fan desperate to touch the hem of the famous writer's garment. If it's an encounter that demonstrates how recognised he had become, it also offered a graphic illustration of something else. As was now all too regularly the case, Behan was too ridiculously drunk to even engage the stranger with the nasal twang to his voice. Perhaps it was just as well.

"Folk-singers, I personally detest," wrote Behan later. "I would shoot every one of them..."

For all that bravura, he was actually no stranger to the venues where a generation of folk singers in New York were honing their acts and changing musical history at this time. Among them were his compatriots Tommy Makem and Liam Clancy, who would become a lot friendlier with Dylan. If that duo were also regulars in The White Horse, Izzy Young, another legendary figure in the music scene, witnessed an evening at the Folklore Centre on MacDougall Street when Makem and Behan exchanged Irish songs and opinions long into the night.

"As Brendan's spirits rose," wrote Young, "so did the earthiness of his songs. Rarely-heard IRA and workers' songs filled the room amidst the approbation of ladies and clergymen present."

The Behan rampaging through the city and burnishing the Falstaffian side of his legend at every turn was far removed from the sober, reformed character portrayed in a lengthy interview with Thomas Quinn Curtiss in the New York Herald Tribune on February 25th. Quinn Curtiss, the newspaper's European-based theatre critic, took advantage of a trip back to New York to sit down with Behan, ahead of the forthcoming premiere at the Theatre de France in Paris of a French translation of "The Hostage". They met in a Chinese restaurant in midtown and

Behan drank so many cups of tea during the meal that the journalist got the completely wrong idea about where his life was heading.

"As Behan's alcoholic exploits have occupied much space on front pages, he is better known to Americans for his drinking than he is for his thinking or his theatrical accomplishments," wrote Quinn Curtiss. "That he is now on the wagon – drinking only orange juice, soda water and tea – is probably surprising and disappointing to those who have revelled in accounts of his stage-Irishman antics. His scenes in public, alas, have attracted a wider audience than the excellent scenes in his plays. But perhaps the tide has turned. 'The Hostage' is enjoying success off-Broadway and he has put the bottle away and gone back to the typewriter."

It wasn't Quinn Curtiss's fault. Behan did his best to persuade him abstinence was the way of it now, claiming his daily routine in New York consisted of writing in the morning, spending the afternoon with friends and attending shows in the evening. He mentioned his admiration of Bertolt Brecht (to whom one French critic had compared him), talked up his progress on "Richard's Cork Leg", and name-dropped an especially convincing story to back up the new abstemious image he was trying to convey.

"I telephoned (Sean) O'Casey before coming over," said Behan. "He told me to stop drinking. 'Why?' I asked. 'Because you have work to do,' he replied. I think he's right."

O'Casey was right but Behan was lying about how seriously he'd taken the advice. Things got so bad during what was just a one-month stay in New York that those around him grew very concerned at the pace of his deterioration. Bernard Geis and Letty Cottin Pogrebin at his publishers, Jack and Viola Lipsett at the Monte Rosa, Perry Bruskin at the theatre, and even Mae, an Irishwoman who worked the telephone exchange at the

Bristol, all tried to persuade him to join AA and/or attempt some sort of rehabilitation. To no avail.

His only sop to addressing his failing health was to meet with Dr. Alter Weiss, a physician to whom he'd been recommended by Bruskin. Having rebuffed a suggestion by Weiss that he required in-patient care, Behan agreed to a regimen of medication. Of course, this probably wasn't the wisest course of action. Behan was in the midst of such an extended bender that he often forgot to put on clothes before going down to the hotel lobby. How was he ever going to remember vials of pills that were supposed to be taken at certain intervals each day?

Weiss also beseeched Arthurs, Behan's constant companion during this trip, to make sure his friend got as much physical exercise as possible. Aside from the regular swims, Arthurs brought Behan to the gym at the McBurney YMCA on 23rd Street. A former boxer himself, Arthurs put the patient to work hitting the heavy bag. It wasn't as preposterous a move as it might have sounded. Behan, too, had boxed and he was on first-name terms with some great boxers. He counted Jack Dempsey and Gene Tunney among the many "friends" he had made since first arriving in New York.

"I used to box at nine stone and two," he told one interviewer of his experience in Borstal as a teenager. "I wasn't a very good boxer. Gene Tunney, who was perhaps the greatest boxer that ever lived, was the only man who ever looked at me and accepted the fact. He said, 'Yeah.' He says, 'Yeah.' Other people say, 'Oh I'm sure you were better than you think you were. You're just saying that. You're just being modest.' Well, I was a very bad boxer for two reasons. I couldn't fight except I was in a temper, and I don't get in a temper unless I get scared. And when I was in the ring I wasn't scared. I guess I wasn't ferocious enough. Basically, I had a short reach — too short a reach for my weight, do you understand?"

Now, he was nowhere nine stone and two. He was overweight, diabetic, and doing just about everything to exacerbate both those conditions. Yet, his star was still bright enough to bring actors and editors to his door, wanting to collaborate. Esquire magazine had asked him to sketch a self-portrait and accompanying essay for their February, 1962 edition. It appeared opposite a similar contribution from the Italian director Federico Fellini. Yet another barometer of what those driving the culture thought of him, the format required him to answer pre-set questions and his answers are revealing.

Asked what was his mainspring, he replied: "All answers except the work itself are sentimental, but I suppose I think that man's short life is often sad and his end disgusting, but he has been a good trier and will improve things."

And was there anything in which he took secret satisfaction? "That I am so highly respected as a writer in Scandinavia, France, Holland, Italy and Finland where my 'reputation' as a boozer is unknown, and that I am respected as a writer in New York and San Francisco, but also receive a great measure of affection from the ordinary people of the US where it is known. This affection I return. God love and guard you all – especially you who will only read this in a dentist's waiting room – Shalom! Sláinte!"

Others still thought he had something to contribute too. Following up on conversations had in Hollywood the previous summer, Andy Pollette, a producer, came to town that month to try to revive the proposed movie version of "Borstal Boy" starring Sal Mineo. Although Behan had boasted upon returning from California about doing a screenplay for Mineo, and there had been press reports of it, he hadn't written a word since.

"Pollette hung around for a few trying days but finally gave up in despair," wrote Arthurs. "Prior to his departure he assured me that my immediate future would be financially secured if I could get Brendan's name on a few sheets of typing paper. The Hollywood screenwriters would fill in the rest. I thoroughly assured him, 'I will do my damndest.' Unfortunately for both of us, he returned to Hollywood without the cherished papers."

If the reality of his professional life was chaos and a lengthening litany of missed opportunities, Behan continued, somehow, to garner good press. The New York Times' theatre section ran a piece about how busy he was. Apart from writing the follow-up memoir to "Borstal Boy" for Geis, and finishing "Richard's Cork Leg" for his eager public, he told journalist Lewis Funke of his plans to start a New York theatre workshop with Bruskin. Loosely based on the model put together by Joan Littlewood in London, the idea was that Behan would come up with an outline and the bones of a play and their company of players would workshop the material into a polished production. Not that implausible a notion except for the small matter that he was busy drinking himself to death.

Amid all the chaos, Behan did a good turn for an old friend. Reginald Gray had been best man when Brendan and Beatrice married at Donnybrook Church that morning back in 1955. Gray had studied under Beatrice's father, the painter Cecil ffrench-Salkeld, and had dated her sister Celia. Now establishing a reputation as an artist in his own right, Behan co-sponsored the first New York exhibition of Gray's work at the Caravan Gallery, his involvement alone generating press for the event. That the best man at the wedding was making his New York debut was particularly poignant because the marriage itself had never been in worst shape.

In the weeks since his untimely departure, Beatrice resisted the urge to follow him across the Atlantic but had, through various means, been trying to effect his return. She'd written to Bruskin to ask for his help in getting her husband back to Dublin, and she'd phoned The Bristol regularly. Brendan usually avoided the calls, unwilling or afraid to speak to her. Arthurs often picked up the receiver and found himself in the middle of an extraordinary marital spat. Beatrice was on the line begging him to do what he could to get Brendan on to the next plane home. Meanwhile, Brendan was standing alongside him whispering instructions in his ear about trying to get Beatrice to come to New York.

"Because she understood Brendan and had made allowances for him as a writer, recognising the sensitive poet under the roaring boy, there was a bond between them until this point that only they understood," wrote Ulick O'Connor, the original Behan biographer, of the state of the marriage by this juncture. "But now she felt betrayed because not only had a friend (Valerie Danby-Smith) behaved treacherously, but Brendan had helped to make her look a fool in front of the very person who had lured him away from her. It was another link gone in the chain that bound Beatrice to Brendan – a link that up to now had prevented him from falling headlong into complete despair and destruction."

Beatrice also enlisted the help of others to try to resolve this bizarre state of affairs, asking Rae Jeffs, Brendan's editor in London, to call New York to advise him to return to Dublin. Jeffs had her own reasons for needing to track him down. She was busy trying to edit the unfinished manuscript of "Brendan Behan's Island," a book of his observations about Ireland that was proving almost impossible to finish because, as she put it, "I was having my own troubles trying to produce a book by a living author who, for all intents and purposes, might have been dead."

This was an alarming yet accurate appraisal of the point his literary career had reached. Here was Jeffs, a publishing veteran whose commitment to the Behan oeuvre had always gone above and beyond the call of her professional duty, admitting that by early 1962, the writer, though not yet 40, was effectively a spent force. Although Arthurs witnessed him fitfully adding pages to "Richard's Cork Leg" at the Bristol, he was somebody almost incapable of sitting down to write coherently anymore.

Jeffs had more than philanthropy on her mind then. To her fell the job of convincing Behan over in New York to allow his publishers Hutchinson to pad out the insufficient book with short stories and poems, and the assistance of Valentin Iremonger, an Irish diplomat, poet and editor.

"He answered the telephone himself and from the tone of his response, I sensed he was suspicious as to how I had traced him," wrote Jeffs. "I would not say he was drunk, but either he had been drinking and was suffering from a hangover or else he was ill. I explained that Val and I were editing his book and he whispered, 'That's good', or words to that effect. Briefly, I mentioned the lack of text and listed the pieces which I hoped he would allow us to include. He would leave the choice entirely to me, he replied wearily, and he sounded so sad and depressed that I asked him why he didn't leave New York and take the next plane home."

His answer to that query was to ask Jeffs how Beatrice was doing. When Jeffs pointed out the absurdity of him in New York asking somebody in London how his wife was doing in Dublin, he had no response. Before the call ended, he requested that Jeffs tell Beatrice he was asking after her. A few days later, he arrived back into Dublin with predictably fiery results but even in his absence, he was still impacting in America.

Leonard Lyons, constantly flying the flag, assured his readers Behan would be back when the weather improved because he'd contracted to make several "summer stock appearances in 'The Hostage'." That he was in no condition to ever fulfil those type of obligations was neither here nor there.

After Behan had left, Arthurs discovered he had quit town without paying up his bill at the Bristol or at the Monte Rosa Restaurant. As his perceived next of kin, Arthurs was expected to make up the shortfall. The veracity of that story can be backed up by the experience of Paul Hogarth, the English artist who'd supplied the sketches for "Brendan Behan's Island". When Hogarth eventually came to Manhattan to sketch Behan's favourite aunts for "Brendan Behan's New York", a later book designed to cash in on his fame in the city, he was accosted in more than one establishment by bartenders seeking to have him pay up Behan's outstanding tabs.

Once out of the country, he left other bills go unpaid too.

"Brendan assured me there would be no difficulty about his supporting [Valerie] and his namesake but the erratic hurly-burly of his life both in New York and in Dublin made it hard for him to keep his word; the money, if it came at all, came by fits and starts," wrote Brendan Gill. "[Valerie] and little Brendan were living in a dark little basement apartment on the West Side of Manhattan; while she was at work in midtown, Brendan was cared for by the Puerto Rican superintendent of the building and his family and so came to speak excellent Spanish before he spoke a word of English."

Gill was very good friends with Danby-Smith and, more than once, she asked him to call Behan in Dublin to remind him of his promise to support his child in New York. An intermediary was necessary, of course, because there was every chance Beatrice would answer the phone in Anglesea Road. Gill's relationship with Behan became an inevitable casualty of this arrangement, the American who once brought him to restaurants and clubs turning into a voice "reminding him of an obligation that he had failed to live up to."

Of course, none of that was public knowledge, and in Behan's absence, his American legend continued to be amplified in the most unlikely and unflattering way when he was the very obvious inspiration for "The Roaring Boy-O", the March 16th episode of "Dr. Kildare", then one of the most popular television shows in the country.

The storyline centred on the misadventures of an Irish poet called Johnny McHenry, a very thinly-disguised caricature of the playwright. The character was played by Dan O'Herlihy, an Irish actor described in the press clippings as a boyhood pal of Behan. The pair had hung out in Hollywood the previous summer and O'Herlihy was perfectly cast as a wise-cracking drunken poet from Dublin who ends up in Dr. Kildare's hospital after a pub brawl (a plot ripped straight from the newspaper headlines generated by Behan in Los Angeles.) There, he complains about the lack of drink and the side-effects of too many sedatives before absconding from the hospital.

Essentially and arguably most disturbingly, the fictive poet's real issue with the drink is that he drinks because he can no longer write. It was just as well then Behan had left the country before the broadcast because this was eerily close to home for a man whose creative well had either run dry or been flooded by alcohol. At the end of the episode, McHenry decides to cut his long-suffering girlfriend free so he can drink himself to death. "Well," smiles Dr. Leonard Gillespie (Raymond Massey) playing Dr. Kildare's boss, "we can't win them all."

Art imitating life that would eventually imitate art.

CHAPTER FIFTEEN

They Remember You Well At The Chelsea Hotel

The other night Brendan Behan phoned Jim Downey's bar on 8th Avenue. Behan was calling from a Dublin rest home. He asked Downey: "Just look down towards Times Square and tell me – are the lights still bright and the hearts still warm?"

LEONARD LYONS, READING EAGLE, OCTOBER 17, 1962

AFTER departing New York in March, 1962, Behan returned to Beatrice in Dublin and to the harsh reality of his increasingly chaotic and troubled life. Over the course of the next 11 months, he spent several stints in hospitals, underwent an operation for a diabetes-related penis infection and refused to undergo brain surgery. Like their counterparts in Toronto, doctors in London wanted to try to alleviate the pressure on his brain but he wasn't having any of it. He sought refuge in the quiet of Connemara and in a farmhouse near Nice, became embroiled in a legal action arising out of the freshly-published "Brendan Behan's Island", and, aside from when billeted in hospital or confined to jail cells, he drank excessively.

At one point he was in such a sorry state on the streets of London that he wandered into a rehab clinic by accident and stayed. His health was so bad – one particular night there was talk of calling a priest to administer the last rites – he agreed to aversion therapy. This involved doctors putting him on drugs that would cause extreme vomiting if he drank with them in his system. For a while he adhered to this regimen but eventually he returned to his old ways. The sojourn in the south of France degenerated into a wine binge that culminated in yet another fight and arrest. When Beatrice confronted him and asked him to choose between her and the bottle, he gave her the answer she feared.

By the end of 1962, he was spending more and more time at the Behan family home in Crumlin rather than the couple's house on Anglesea Road. Most ominously of all, he talked constantly about his desire to go back to America. During some of these conversations, Brendan mentioned how he wished to return to resume treatment with Dr. Alter Weiss. He wasn't to know that Weiss had died in the meantime. In any case, given his morbid fear and distrust of doctors, his real reason for wanting to get back to New York may have had more to do with Valerie and baby Brendan than with his desire to meet up with a physician he liked.

This much can be surmised from the fact he was placing transatlantic phone calls with such frequency and ferocity when dealing with the operators that the Department of Post and Telegraphs disconnected the Behans' line. Once too often, he had been abusive to those charged with putting the calls through. Not the type of phone calls somebody makes to a doctor's office, even one 3000 miles away. Much more like the actions of a man trying to contact the mother of his son under strained circumstances.

"Brendan was more restless than I had ever known him and was decidedly unhappy in Dublin," wrote Beatrice. "So it was my mother who was surprised one afternoon to get a call from Brendan asking her to convey a message to me. He was at London airport, he said, on his way to New York."

Exactly like the previous year, he travelled in the clothes he stood up in. Spur of the moment. On a whim. Or maybe he was a man just too afraid to tell his wife where he was going and why he was going there. In any case, he arrived in New York in the last week of February, 1963 and checked into a room on the fourth floor of the Bristol Hotel. Peter Arthurs, recently injured in an accident on an oil tanker, was already a guest at the establishment, recuperating from his injuries. When he first bumped into Behan upon his arrival, he found him in the company of a lawyer claiming to be acting for Valerie Danby-Smith and Brendan junior in the matter of the unpaid child support. If that encounter with a legal eagle left Behan paranoid about his situation for days, it was the condition of his old friend that shocked Arthurs.

"At the age of 40, he was a weather-beaten curio, an ancient drayhorse," wrote Arthurs of what had happened to Behan in the year since he'd last seen him. "His eyes became increasingly gargoylish, his battered countenance twisted into a rictus; Brendan was a desiccated wreck...Staggering around 48th Street, he looked like a decayed sorcerer on his way to a black mass. Gone was his poetry. Beleaguered by fatherhood worries and creative aridity, he turned to anyone who would lend him a thin ear."

His friends in New York were surprised at his arrival, nobody more so than Bernard Geis when Behan called to his apartment early one Sunday morning. That it was rather a strange hour to be paying a house call didn't bother Geis unduly, not when Behan assured him he'd come to the city at such short notice because he wanted to get writing. As somebody who'd signed Behan to a three-book deal, Geis was delighted to hear this. At least initially. After a while, once Brendan had suggested they toast his arrival with something from the drinks cabinet, it became apparent that the real reason for the visit was more personal than professional, more to do with whiskey than writing.

In Manhattan, the bars weren't open on Sunday until noon. Behan sought to get around that law by dropping in on a publisher he presumed would be so happy to see him that the drink might flow, even before midday. To his credit, Geis refused to give in to the pleading to break out a bottle of something or other. Behan kept up the campaign but the host wouldn't budge. Eventually, Brendan noticed the clock was five minutes away from 12. By the time he got back downstairs on the street, the bars would be open. He made his excuses and left. In a hurry.

"We had some conversation in his rambling discursive way," wrote Geis of the encounter. "He claims he is going to finish 'Confessions of an Irish Rebel' soon but I'll believe that when it happens. I'm going to give him the initial portion of the MS and try to set him up in the office so that he can work on the book every day. While he heartily agrees to this plan, it will be a small miracle if it materialises. Yesterday, for example, he called me to say he was on his way to the office, but he never showed up."

In truth, the audience for the one-man show he seemed to put on in every New York pub he ever visited was dwindling. Many of the establishments he'd treated as second homes during previous stays now shut their doors to him. He was in such a parlous state that his custom simply wasn't worth the trouble. The manager of the Bristol Hotel decided as much too. After one too many naked jaunts through the lobby, Behan was asked to check out. Getting evicted from the historic Algonquin Hotel was one thing, being shown the door at a place Arthurs called "cockroach junction", well that was something else altogether. Things had reached a very sorry pass.

After being shown the door at the Bristol that March morning, he arrived at Geis's office in such a terrible condition that the publisher seriously considered having him committed to Bellevue Psychiatric Hospital. Behan was spared this ordeal only by the intervention of Katherine Dunham. So famous in her own right as a choreographer and dancer that some regard her as "the queen mother of black dance", Dunham made a suggestion.

"Why not move him into the Chelsea?" she asked. "I'll keep an eye on him."

The Chelsea was at 222 West 23rd Street, between 7th and 8th Avenues. Dunham lived there, along with several members of her dance company. She believed this extended family could, for a fee, keep an eye on the poor man who appeared at his wit's end. An extraordinary offer? Certainly. But, she was quite an extraordinary woman. During her stay at the hotel, she'd once asked the management if it was okay to conduct rehearsals for a forthcoming Metropolitan Opera production of Aida in her room. They agreed until, in the interests of authenticity, she walked through the lobby and onto the elevator with two lions roaring at the other guests.

"Dunham had spent her life rescuing artists from dire straits, training them professionally, and providing them with classes in anthropology, philosophy and languages, as well as in dance and theatre," wrote Sherill Tippins in a biography of the hotel itself. "It was an easy matter, then, for her to nurse a simple alcoholic like Behan back to health."

The move to the Chelsea was not without complications. For a start, the management team there, David Bard and his son Stanley, were no fools. They'd seen the newspaper reports about Behan. They'd heard the legion of stories from restaurant owners and bartenders around town about his antics. It took all the persuasive powers in Geis's not inconsiderable arsenal to convince them that they owed it to the heritage of this historic hotel, long the haven of eccentric and troubled artists, to take in this tormented creative soul, like they had so many before him, in his hour of need.

"There is a plaque to his [Dylan Thomas] memory outside the Hotel Chelsea on which there are also the names of Arthur B. Davies, James T. Farrell, Robert Flaherty, O. Henry, John Sloan, Thomas Wolfe and Edgar Lee Masters," wrote Behan of his arrival in this storied institution, showing he was fully aware of the place's history. "I would hope that Mr. Bard, the proprietor, and his son Stanley, who has a beautiful baby daughter, would leave space on their plaque for myself. I am not humble enough to say that I do not deserve one, but I hope it does not come too soon...."

Behan was initially put into a room across from Dunham's and, with the help of her dancers, they had him on a strict regime. He was plied with milk and apple juice as they began trying to nurse him back towards some sort of health. That he had some distance to go is captured in the first impression he made on Arthur Miller, another resident.

"Later, there was another who came to the Chelsea to die, the Borstal boy himself, Brendan Behan, on his last legs then, asking me to come to the room where Katherine Dunham had put him up..." wrote Miller. "He sat there, his wet hair haphazardly plastered down, his face blotched, lisping through broken teeth, laughing and eating sausages and eggs while black dancers moved in and out of the room, not knowing how to help him or whether even tenderly to try..."

Once he was strong enough, he was allowed down to the lobby for a brief spell every afternoon to mix with the rest of the guests and to stave off cabin fever. Pretty soon, he had recovered some of his usual brio. He started to put back on some of the weight he'd lost. Eventually, he was back to making a genuine nuisance of himself, constantly dropping down to Miller's room to use the phone to call Ireland, and causing a stir wherever he went.

"You couldn't imagine anyone giving the hotel such a jolt," said Dunham. "The maid wouldn't go into his room unless he agreed to put on clothes and stop chasing her. His singing and doing jigs was amusing but a little of it went a long way. And down the hall there was a lady who kept locking herself out of her room with hardly any clothes, saying, 'Excuse me, I really belong in a nudist colony.'"

At last, he had found a place where on any given day he wasn't even the loosest cannon in the arsenal. This was a community of eccentrics where, in so many ways, he fit right in. Residents quickly became used to the soundtrack of Behan singing at the top of his voice, in corridors, in elevators and in the lobby, one more addition to the bizarre cacophony of the place.

Inevitably, he was drawn to Elizabeth Gurley Flynn, the daughter of Irish emigrants. By that time in a remarkable life, Gurley Flynn was 73 years old, and the chairwoman of the Communist Party of the USA which often met in her room. A one-time contemporary of Jim Larkin in the labour struggle, she'd been agitating for women's and worker's rights for decades, was involved in the founding of the American Civil Liberties Union, and served time in prison for anti-government activity. The sort of epic biography that, once upon a time, might have inspired Behan to write. Now, he just acted the fool around her.

"Gurley, you're the only Irish-American I know who's worth anything!" he'd roar as he lifted her clean off the floor, before dancing along the hallways with her.

George Kleinsinger became another fast friend. A composer who'd collaborated with Mel Brooks, he'd written, amongst other things, one smash-hit song called "Tubby the Tuba". He lived on the 10th floor in a penthouse studio that he'd turned into a forest with 12 foot trees imported from Borneo and Madagascar that played host to a menagerie of creatures. At various times, Kleinsinger shared his room with iguanas, turtles, a boa constrictor, a python, a basilisk, a gecko, and a flock of assorted birds. No hotel in the world would have tolerated a tropical zoo in its midst. Except the Chelsea.

The first time Behan went into Kleinsinger's room, he burst into song, and a mynah bird began to chirp along. Behan stopped singing rather abruptly and roared: "Stop the competition." It was a routine he'd repeat nearly every time he stopped by thereafter. And that was a lot because the writer and the composer bonded over their mutual love of music. When he finally broke loose of the restrictions placed upon him by Dunham, he liked to hang out in Kleinsinger's room where, apart from the animals, he was fascinated by a large framed photograph of Charlie Chaplin sitting in a bath, wearing a suit.

As was now traditionally the case, the initial stay at the Chelsea was the quiet before the storm. When he was back on his feet, Dunham began giving him five dollars spending money each morning, enough to carry him through the day without quite financing a binge. A reasonable assumption except she was dealing with an alcoholic with a proven talent for coaxing free drink from fellow drinkers and bartenders. No to mention Peter Arthurs, who'd initially been kept away by Dunham before she realised how close the two men were, was also giving Behan cash each day.

Eventually, once he was somewhat back to normal (as normal as he got at this stage of his life), he was considered well enough to mix in polite society again. He was booked to appear on a radio show called "Monitor", hosted by a character called Fitzgerald Smith. The location for the interview was NBC Studios in Rockefeller Centre where many of the recording rooms are glass-walled and fronting onto the street. At one point during the chat – the reason for his visit was to promote the forthcoming "Brendan Behan's Ireland" – Behan saw a gaggle of people standing outside, staring through the glass.

"Who the devil are all these people?" he asked.

"Tourists," said Smith.

"I'll give them something to look at," said Behan, with a glint in his eye. His jacket came off first. Then he slipped his braces down, and as he did, his pants fell to the floor, leaving him standing there with a shirt hanging down over his underpants. On the other side of the glass stood some now-horrified onlookers. Smith was mortified and, off in the wings, his publicist Letty Cottin Pogrebin didn't know where to look.

That incident marked his return to the gossip columns after a brief hiatus. Similarly, an innocuous encounter with a writer called Eileen Bassing provided more fodder for the papers. Bassing had just published "Where's Annie?" and while in New York to promote what would become a best-seller, she bumped into Behan at Sardi's. Later, she told reporters she was appalled that the Irishman didn't rise out of his chair when she came over to his table. She was more appalled when he spent much of their subsequent conversation staring at her décolletage and making comments about her lacey brassiere.

There were other incidents too. When Letty Cottin Pogrebin brought her fiancée to meet Behan, they witnessed a minor explosion.

"We went for drinks in a bar, a few doors from the Chelsea. Brendan was delightful company and very pleased with my choice of partner," said Pogrebin. "In the course of our chat, a wreck of a woman (smudged make-up, slurred speech, rat's nest hairdo) came over to our table and began berating him for some perceived slight. Instead of being embarrassed, Brendan let loose a barrage of crude profanities, calling the poor woman everything from 'an old whore' to 'a dried-up cunt.' My husband tells that story to this day, and it was 50 years ago."

At this time, Geis published "On the Road for Uncle Sam", a memoir by popular comedian Joey Adams about his time touring the world as part of a US State Department-sponsored goodwill tour. Geis asked Behan to the launch party, not knowing he'd been drinking in his room with Peter Arthurs for much of the day. Before a who's who of New York society, Behan grabbed a microphone and launched into a drunken attempt at comedy.

Within seconds, Adams was begging Geis to get him out.

These type of incidents aside, once Behan was approaching some sort of fitness, there arose the issue of work and completing the outstanding book contracts for which Geis had advanced him $15,000. "Brendan Behan's Island" had been produced in collaboration with his editor Rae Jeffs over the course of a few weeks back in January, 1960. Jeffs, then publicity director at the London publishers Hutchinson, went to Dublin with a tape recorder on which she recorded the conversations that became the manuscript. It wasn't ideal but three years on, he was having difficulty holding a pencil in his hand, so Geis phoned Jeffs at home in England. Could she "magic" a book from their conversations again?

On April 9th, 1963, Jeffs arrived in New York with her daughter Diana. When she met Brendan outside the Chelsea later that day, she was pleasantly surprised at how well he looked, wearing a dazzling white shirt and a pair of trousers that looked like they'd been pressed rather than slept in. He expressed concern that working with him was going to keep her from her daughter, warned them both that New York was a more dangerous spot than London or Paris, and then he decided to play tour guide. This cameo offered a glimpse into the man-child side of his character, showing off a city he'd come to regard as his own private plaything.

He was in ebullient form, assuring them he'd be the perfect guide around the town, and unspooling stories and yarns as they went. He'd recently been the drunken victim of a mugging off Third Avenue, losing money and his passport, but no harm. He told the Jeffs how chuffed he was that while applying for his new passport at the Irish embassy, an official waived the statutory need for him to prove his nationality. More proof of his legend, grist for his mill.

"For the next few days, Brendan introduced us to the city

which he had come to regard as his second home, pointing out the famous landmarks with an air of lairdship," wrote Jeffs. "He took an almost childish pleasure in Diana's excitement and wonder. Whether he was giving us the background to the building of the Statue of Liberty, showing us his favourite churches and their links with his own country, walking down Broadway, praising the neon lights and the friendliness they generated, or speeding through the Bowery – a district he particularly detested as he had once been marooned in it – he was a rare companion, and his main thought was always that we should be enjoying ourselves."

The sight of Behan around town in the company of a new woman drew attention. Any murmurs or whispers about the nature of their relationship were put to bed quickly when the newspapers learned her identity. "Woman Boswell to follow Behan" was one headline over a story in which she explained that she'd come to New York to help him finish his autobiography.

"I'll try to be with him whenever possible – at parties, in saloons – places where Brendan can expect to do some talking," said Jeffs in one interview "By the time I'm through I expect to have 100,000 words – all Brendan's. Then, he can take the transcription – read it and sit down and do the heavy work. A jolly way to write a book, don't you think?"

There are two things here. The level of his fame was such that this was the lead item in a nationally-syndicated column. It was also a very frank and public admission by Jeffs and Geis (the man with the most money invested) that Behan the functioning writer was effectively shot even if his thoughts, reminisces and observations retained value. That they were willing to be this honest about the modus operandi sums up how far he'd fallen. There wasn't even an attempt at a pretence.

Behan was equally open about the situation. Arthur Miller recalled a conversation during which he said: "I'm not really a playwright, you know – and you'd know that of course – I'm a talker." He also claimed that Jeffs had been set upon him by publishers desperate to recoup their investment and he was merely going along with the arrangement in the hope they'd "empty another purse over me head."

For all that bravado, meeting the likes of Miller in the hotel brought home to him what an historic institution the Chelsea was, and in his most vulnerable moments, he regarded himself as inferior to some of the past residents.

"He felt himself a subway sweep compared to Dylan Thomas and Thomas Wolfe," said Letty Cottin Pogrebin.

There was a genuinely elegiac tone to this latest and last sojourn in New York. Sean Callery had known Behan since 1945 but, with both of them now transplanted to Manhattan, his most poignant memory of Behan at this time centres on mornings in Costello's on Third Avenue. Sometimes the bartender Honest John Gallagher would be driven to work by a friend of his who worked as a house-painter. If Brendan was among the crowd gathered outside waiting for the doors to open, and the cures to be administered, he'd immediately gravitate towards the painter.

"He and John's house-painter friend repaired to a booth and traded opinions on the techniques of plastering and mixing, and swapped stories of housewives they had dallied with while the first coat was drying on the walls. It was the closest he got to the not-so-bad old days."

There was something else to consider too. The Chelsea was where Dylan Thomas had been living when he, essentially, drank himself to death in November, 1953. Doctors at St. Vincent's Hospital concluded that the Welsh poet had consumed so much straight scotch (some accounts put it at 18 straight) that he suffered "insult to the brain". He was 39 when he died. Here was Behan knocking around the very same corridors, just turned 40, and in a similarly debilitated condition.

"Brendan was aware that I had known Dylan Thomas and that I feared, as Brendan approached the age at which Thomas died, he might suffer a similar grotesque fate," wrote Brendan Gill. "...Brendan was engaged in massively insulting his brain, in a way that even his exceptionally strong constitution could not long withstand. I would plead with him to seek medical attention for his alcoholism and he would say jeeringly, 'Ah, you think I'll be pulling a Thomas on you, but I won't. Remember, I have a Swiss bank account and nobody with a Swiss bank account has ever died young.' Whether Brendan had a Swiss bank account I was never to learn..."

CHAPTER SIXTEEN

Give My Regards To Broadway

Perhaps the last Hemingway hero was Brendan Behan...Unfortunately, his sudden late flowering made him the victim of a society, and of some circles within it, where he could be engaged to provide the stimulus, necessary to jaded appetites, of the exotic. For those he soon found himself performing the functions of dancing bear and court jester, only to be dropped when they found a new fad, and one less likely to smash their furniture and urinate on their doorsteps when they had plied him with too much drink.

BERNARD LEVIN, RUN IT DOWN THE FLAGPOLE

IT is a credit to Rae Jeffs' professionalism and, perhaps to Behan's trust in her, that she somehow forced him to sit still long enough over the coming weeks to start taping what would eventually become "Confessions of an Irish Rebel". She rented a tape recorder from a shop on 7th Avenue and sometimes she would have to set it up in the bedroom of his apartment at the Chelsea so the interview could be conducted with him lying in bed. Other times, he'd call her at six in the morning because he'd thought of something he wanted to include and needed her to record it while it was fresh in his mind.

Although he occasionally responded to her initial questions with long periods of silence, he was also capable of unleashing great torrents of words when the mood or the inspiration struck him. He was committed enough to the process to even re-record long sessions when the machine malfunctioned and material was lost. In this bizarre way, they managed, within a fortnight, to get 50,000 words down on paper. The work was done with nobody else in the room and in those private moments, he often deviated from the reminiscing at hand to talk about Beatrice and his troubled marriage. He confessed to missing his wife and to being very ashamed of the clandestine manner in which he'd left her in Dublin.

Since the phone line had been disconnected at the house on Anglesea Road because of his repeated abuse of operators, there was no way for him to call Beatrice directly. He did phone her parents, beseeching them to persuade her to come to America. During one call, the ffrench-Salkelds told him Beatrice had booked her passage to New York and was due to arrive on April 20. Before that ominous date, he had another esteemed visitor in Kenneth Allsop, a writer, broadcaster and critic with the Daily Mail. Behan thought enough of Allsop that he, Jeffs and her daughter went to Idlewild to meet his plane and to welcome him to the city.

Mostly, he put on his best face for Allsop, determined to keep up appearances for a gentleman of the English press. In truth though, he was panicking inside about the impending arrival of his wife. The day she was scheduled to leave England, he insisted that Jeffs phone the ffrench-Salkelds to check whether she had actually set sail. When they confirmed she had, he prepared for her visit by upping his consumption levels, getting drunker and drunker each successive day. His anxiety was no doubt exacerbated by the fact the coming of his wife meant steps had to be taken to remove Valerie and baby Brendan from the room they had begun sharing with him at the Chelsea.

On the morning of April 20th, the Queen Elizabeth pulled into Pier 90 with Beatrice Behan on board. Unlike with Allsop, Behan didn't bother to go to meet her. He was able to make the trip to the airport to greet a critic from London alright but he couldn't catch a cab a few blocks across Manhattan from the Chelsea to where the ship carrying his wife docked. When she walked down the gangway, Beatrice scanned the crowd for him in vain The only familiar faces she saw were those of Jeffs and Peter Arthurs. She pretended not to be too disappointed by the absence of her husband while the welcoming committee did their best to assure her all was well.

The moment she set foot in the Chelsea for the first time though, she soon discovered that was not the case. At reception, Beatrice introduced herself to Stanley Bard as Mrs. Brendan Behan and asked to be shown to her room. Bard gave her an odd look then brought her up in the elevator and opened the door to a suite that contained a vase of fresh flowers but no sign of her husband or any of his belongings.

"This room isn't occupied," said Beatrice.

"I know that Mrs. Behan," said Bard. "But aren't you instituting divorce proceedings against your husband?"

"Well if I'm getting divorced, it's the first I've heard of it," she replied. "Please take me to Mr. Behan's room."

In truth, the hotelier was only going on what he'd heard from a lot of people around the Chelsea, including Brendan himself. Not to mention he'd also seen that Valerie had been living there with Brendan and their child. Suitably chastened by Beatrice's response, he led her to the room in which her husband lay asleep in yet another drunken stupor, a half-consumed bottle of Jack Daniels on the pillow next to his head. She sat down in a chair by the window, watched him sleeping and started to wonder, why she had followed him all the way across the Atlantic.

Eventually, Behan started to wake from his slumber, at first struggling to make out exactly who it was sitting in front of him. He knew soon enough. When Beatrice reprimanded him for failing to meet her off the boat, he offered a very honest apology: "Sorry I couldn't get down, I had a terrible fucking hangover!"

Not something she needed to be reminded of as she sat staring at him in this awful condition, looking at her past, her present and, maybe, her future. In the Chelsea that morning, the Behans were forced to finally confront the elephant in the room, the issue of the other woman (not to mention the other man) in their relationship. Brendan confessed all about the nature of his relationship with Valerie and after eight years of marriage, Beatrice talked about how many of her friends had urged her to leave him and move on. Never mind the fact Bard and plenty others had assumed they were already on the way to the divorce courts.

"People used to say to me, 'Why don't you get a divorce?'" said Beatrice. "But he was down at that stage. That wasn't the time to walk out. Perhaps if he had risen to the heights again I might have left then but you don't leave somebody when they are low."

That their life together was a more crowded and complicated place was brought home to Beatrice when she was approached in the hotel by Katherine Dunham and an accountant from Bernard Geis. They presented her with a bill for the money spent on her husband's recuperation over the previous month. It was a professionally put-together reckoning of every cent they'd outlaid from the day it was decided to book him into the Chelsea rather than take him to BelleVue. The total came to just over $1500. Quite a sum considering he'd been strictly supervised for the first couple of weeks of his time on Dunham's watch. In any case, Beatrice refused to pay.

On April 23rd, two months after the actual milestone had passed, Brendan celebrated his 40th birthday at Fellini's in Greenwich Village. "Frankly, I never thought I'd make it," he told reporters of the milestone he had reached. The belated party had been thrown for him by his old friends Bernie Pollack and Beulah Garrick. Unfortunately, the sober and relentlessly charismatic character who'd shared their car journey down the west coast of America two years earlier was long gone. In his stead was a man who inhaled three bottles of red wine at such a pace that he eventually regurgitated most of it, spewing all over Garrick, Pollack, Beatrice and Jeffs.

The following week, Jeffs decided she'd wrung as much material as she could out of Brendan for now and that it was time for her and her daughter to return to England. At their farewell dinner in Downey's, he was more entertaining than messy. Before his voice cracked, he belted out "The Star-Spangled Banner", "La Marseillaise" and even "Land of Hope and Glory". At Pier 90 the next morning however, he cut a dour and uncommunicative figure. It might have been the hangover. It might also have been that he resented her departure, knowing she was now the only way he could get any words down on paper. Without Jeffs, was he even entitled to call himself a writer anymore?

Certainly, the stark difference between the unorthodox work methods and schedule of her husband and the approach of other writers ensconced in the quirky hotel quickly became apparent to Beatrice.

"The Chelsea was an unusual literary enclosure," she wrote. "One assumed that James Baldwin and Arthur Miller and Arthur Clarke were preoccupied somewhere in the hotel with their writing, yet at the same time I suppose I shouldn't have been surprised when a girl in the hotel propositioned me, an encounter which alarmed me but amused Brendan, or that George [Kleinsinger], a kind person, should have befriended a homeless Jamaican girl, abandoned by her boyfriend, until she had her baby, or even that Rae should offer to become the baby's grandmother."

Against that background, it's not surprising that Beatrice kept her biggest bit of news secret from her husband for nearly a fortnight after her arrival. She was two months pregnant. She had told Jeffs as much very soon after stepping off the ship but refrained from informing Brendan, perhaps fearing how he might react to such a life-changing announcement. Indeed, she was so concerned with how he'd take the news that the day Jeffs left for London, she felt it necessary to give Beatrice $20 just in case Brendan threw her out of the Chelsea.

Was that a possible outcome? Absolutely. A man capable of hitting his wife was surely capable of ejecting her from the room they were sharing. This is why Beatrice was predictably nervous about breaking the news of her pregnancy.

At various junctures in their life together, usually when her husband went off the rails, it was suggested to Beatrice that having a baby might force him to live a more sober lifestyle. Notwithstanding the fact this is easier said than done, especially with somebody so in the grip of alcoholism, it was something she'd addressed in public. In an interview two years earlier, when a journalist suggested that a child might settle Brendan down, Beatrice gave her take on that notion.

"Yes I've often thought about that," she said. "But you can't just have a baby in two minutes. How could I go through my pregnancy and look after the baby properly when I have Brendan to look after? He's a full-time job really."

He remained a full-time job. When she finally plucked up the courage to blurt out the news she was carrying his child, he muttered, without any great conviction, the words, "That's great." As he said no more about it thereafter, and his behaviour seemed unaffected by such a seismic announcement, she wondered if he'd actually heard her properly.

"She was convinced that the news did not register immediately and she repeated it again two days later," wrote Michael O'Sullivan. "His reaction was swift and decisive. He went to the lawyers Greenbaum, Wolff and Ersnstbat at 285

Madison Avenue and made his will, leaving his entire estate to Beatrice. The sudden realisation that he was to have a child with Beatrice made him do the first responsible thing he had done in two or three years."

Unfortunately, it was also the last responsible thing he did for some time. Regardless, or some might even say, because of the presence of an expectant wife, Behan spent much of the next few weeks on a protracted binge. He became even more dissolute than usual. Very often, he'd return to their apartment at the Chelsea, battered and bruised, bearing the physical scars of beatings handed out to him by those he offended in bars. That list, of course, was growing longer and longer, every time he set foot on the street.

"He (Behan) would hold forth on the sidewalk outside," wrote Arthur Miller, "the vomit coming up and dripping on his tie as he joked and told his stories and sung a few ditties, rustling meanwhile through a (New York) Post to see if he was in Leonard Lyons again today, the columnists delighting in him now that he would soon be gallantly supplying them with the story of his rousing poet's death."

More than once he was mugged and had his wallet stolen. These types of incidents increased in frequency because he started to frequent rougher and rougher pubs. Why? Well, the establishments where he'd spent much of his previous visits were tired of his antics and his increasingly truculent persona. He now drank mostly in places where the clientele were often pimps and whores. The Silver Rail, the dive bar at the corner of Seventh Avenue and 23rd Street, where Letty Cottin Pogrebin once picked him up off the floor, became a particular favourite spot. One of the assaults he suffered during this period was reputedly committed by a male prostitute he'd just hired. The portrait is very much of a man struggling with his own identity.

"His neighbours stood by helplessly as he took to loitering in front of the hotel in a state of appalling drunkenness, trying to engage passersby in conversation and inviting the ridicule of those who didn't know who he was," wrote Sherill Tippins in her biography of the hotel. "Under the influence of alcohol, he occasionally asked an acquaintance of his to set up an appointment for him with a male prostitute, but then, when the time came for the rendezvous, he inevitably failed to appear."

John Ryan, an old friend from the Dublin literary scene, came to town and was shocked at the condition of Behan when they met.

"As the illness grew, the drinking increased; he was stupefied from both," wrote Ryan. "I had dinner in Jim Downey's Steak House on Eight Avenue, New York, with Beatrice and himself one evening in April, 1963. 'You've come a long way from Mac's studio on Grafton Street where you ate the cat's dinner,' I observed. But he was too sick and tired even to smile. He just sat there like a mound of blubber – or Orson Welles in the last reels of 'Citizen Kane'."

For all that, he remained a box office attraction. People continued to try to cash in on his celebrity by inviting him to openings and launches where he was expected to play the drunken, tormented Irish writer, a turn that would inevitably generate headlines and publicity. He remained on the invite list for exclusive parties around town where the hosts perhaps felt his presence might bring some radical chic to the evening. More than one of those people found out the hard way that once he arrived they got a lot more than they bargained for in terms of his antics.

One weekend, he was driven out to Great Neck on Long Island to be the token celebrity at a fundraiser for SANE, the New York Council for a sane nuclear policy. Less than an hour from Manhattan, he was well out of it by the time he reached the event. Sean Callery, his old friend from Dublin, had been behind that particular invitation. With Peter Arthurs on holiday in Ireland at this time, Beatrice often called on Callery to go looking in the bars for Behan when he went missing in the city.

These types of forays were becoming more and more common. One of those "lost" evenings, he wandered into the Five Spot Café, a jazz club on Third Avenue that was playing host to a six-month residency by the great Thelonious Monk. If the crowd had come to see one of the more avant-garde pianists of the time, they were also treated to a surprising cameo.

"Monk was playing when a drunk got up from the bar and went over to the piano and started singing Irish songs," wrote one eyewitness. "I wondered why the owners of the bar didn't throw the guy out. Then someone said, 'It's Brendan Behan'. So they left him alone to sing Irish songs as Monk improvised modern jazz. Monk did not seem at all upset or surprised."

Behan was in a dishevelled state on the stage. He had one arm draped around the bemused Monk's shoulders, the other was keeping his trousers up because there was a problem with his braces. Eventually, the owners took action, politely escorting him down off the stage and back to his table. There he remained and, according to those in the room, "dug Monk for an hour".

On June 2nd, Behan was invited to appear on "The Open Mind", a Sunday afternoon talk show on NBC where the topic down for discussion was "The Irish in America". The rest of the panel was made up of Cecil Woodham Smith, the Anglo-Irish historian who had indicted the English role in the Great Famine in "The Great Hunger", Vivian Mercier, an associate professor of English at CUNY, and James O'Gara, editor of the Commonweal, a Catholic publication.

O'Gara was an interesting character whose outspoken attacks on Joseph McCarthy had him denounced by some in his own religion as a 'card-carrying communist'. Mercier, an

Offaly-born, graduate of Trinity College in Dublin, had become a prominent academic in various American universities and a Beckettian scholar. The programme was taped on a Saturday afternoon and Behan, inevitably by this point, had a lot of drink on board when the cameras rolled. Yet, he still managed to put up a good show.

"Brendan was drunk and eloquent on the telly and drunk and a little self-satisfied at our table," wrote Sean Callery who watched the broadcast in a bar with the Behans. "Brendan treated Woodham-Smith with something like adoration; one might almost say that he was overcome with emotions of gratitude, respect and empathy."

Behan was much less charitable to Mercier with whom he crossed swords several times during the broadcast, and, in Callery's perhaps not unbiased view, "gave him hell". Given the state he was in mentally and physically, it was some achievement that he didn't let himself down in the studio. By this time, the invitations to appear on the major shows were becoming very rare, his unpredictability now deemed too much of a gamble by producers. Although he didn't know it then, this appearance, not quite four years on from his "Small World" debut, was the last time he'd feature on a serious American television programme.

When not drinking himself into a stupor, Behan could often be found in George Kleinsinger's room, a place he started to treat as a haven from all the madness, conveniently ignoring the fact, of course, that a lot the madness was of his own creation. Initially, they had bonded over their mutual love of song and the room fairly thrummed with music whenever they were together. Behan was often happy just to sit watching the antics of the various animals as Kleinsinger played the piano. Sometimes, Kleinsinger recorded his friend singing tunes from his plays and "Amhran na Bhfiann".

There were nights however when a darkness overcame Behan as he sat with a man who, more than most in the hotel, seemed to have become a genuine friend. Befitting somebody in a parlous physical state who was doing very little to arrest his apparently terminal decline, he confessed his fear of death to Kleinsinger. Even more tellingly, he revealed his insecurities about the quality of the other writers in the Chelsea. He wondered aloud whether or not he was actually a phony who was being found out. It doesn't take a psychoanalyst to figure that no longer being able to write or type anything meaningful with his own hands was destroying him.

Those still seeking to profit from Behan's celebrity saw Kleinsinger as a conduit to him. Rae Jeffs and Beatrice were in the room on Friday, June 14th when somebody phoned and begged Kleinsinger to bring Behan to a party. Beatrice didn't feel up to going but an hour later, her husband was in the middle of a throng in a penthouse apartment on the other side of New York city. He belted out his off-colour ditty "Lady Chatterley's Lover" to the delight of the crowd and the dismay of the host. Not for the first time, somebody seeking Behan's presence to liven up a shindig discovered that could be a double-edged sword. Soon, the gentleman was begging Jeffs and Kleinsinger to take Behan away.

The sight of Behan in full voice that evening lifted Jeffs' spirits. She had returned to New York at the end of May, with the purpose of finishing "Confessions" and started to tape a book of his reflections on Manhattan that would eventually be published as "Brendan Behan's New York". Upon arrival, she had found him to be a shell of himself, constantly withdrawn, lethargic and distant. Here then at last at this party was a glimpse of the old ham, turning it on for the audience. It was to prove a fleeting glimpse. That night, like so many others, deteriorated into drunken carnage.

Having divested himself of his companions on the way back to the Chelsea, he embarked on a pub crawl and ended up having to be helped up to his room by the hotel porter. He spent the following day shuttling from his bed to the bathroom, vomiting violently. By Sunday morning, there was some improvement. He was no longer throwing up and seemed capable of speech again.

This was the scene when Jeffs knocked at the door to check up on him. Her arrival offered Beatrice the chance to seek some fresh air and a break from playing nurse to an ailing drunk, hardly the best occupation for a pregnant woman. It was then, unprompted, that Behan started to talk about the drink, its place in his life and the growing realisation it was ruining him, his talent and his relationships. To Jeffs, his tone was almost apologetic as he admitted he was desperate to try, for once and for all, to address the problem of what she described, rather quaintly, as his "appalling thirst".

This epiphany may or may not have been occasioned by an advertisement in that day's New York Times for a book called "Drink and Stay Sober" by Eudora Ramsay Richardson and Josiah Pitts Woolfolk. Whether the unusual moment of clarity came due to physical pain or because his eye was taken by this self-help manual (already a decade in print by then), he decided, as a matter of urgency, he needed a copy of this tome. Reading this, he believed, would be the start of the end of his drinking days. He knew of a bookstore in Greenwich Village that opened on Sundays and he begged Jeffs to go and buy the book. His new abstemiousness just couldn't wait.

"Although I seriously doubted whether he was able to read in his present state," wrote Jeffs. "his manner of asking me so resembled the plight of a shipwrecked man who is clasping at a life-belt that I could not refuse."

By the time Beatrice returned from taking the air, Behan was asleep and the two women went off on the book-hunting expedition together. The book proved impossible to find. By the time the two women got back to the room, their chief concern was how the patient might take that disappointing news. Far worse than that awaited them though. When they pushed the door open, he was sitting on the bed with a book in his hand. Hardly an unusual tableau except the book was upside down, the Sunday papers were scattered all over the floor, and some of the pages were now stained with what looked like blood. Worst of all, he didn't even register when they told him of their failure to secure what he'd asked for

Beatrice knew the signs better than Jeffs. She called her colleague out of earshot to tell her it looked like Brendan had had a seizure in their absence. Medical help was required. Fast. Jeffs went to her own room to call a doctor friend she knew. Unfortunately, he was out of the city but when she finally tracked him down, he gave her the name of Dr. Max Tasler. Again, a small comedy of errors ensued involving missing phone calls before the doctor arrived at the hotel just after nine. Behan was sedated but suffered another seizure that required Tasler and Beatrice to hold him down until the worst had passed.

Eventually, an ambulance was called to take him to nearby University Hospital. As the paramedics wheeled Behan out on a stretcher, Peter Arthurs was walking into the lobby, just off the plane at Idlewild following a holiday in Ireland. When he looked over at the pale, lifeless body being carted away, for a moment, he thought it was Behan's corpse.

"He's not dead," said Beatrice. "He's just a little sick."

CHAPTER SEVENTEEN

The Best Wine Makes The Sharpest Vinegar

There always seemed to be small, flashing demons darting around Brendan's head. When sober, he had a lovely, modulated, working-class Dubliner's manner of speech and a not-quite-shy way with him – 'uncertain', I think would be the best way to describe it. The Yahoos and the drink were omnipresent in his life, and it was hard for him to resist the adoration of one and the taste of the other.

MALACHY McCOURT

HAVING slipped into a coma during the night, Brendan Behan woke the next morning in the intensive care ward of New York's University Hospital but his mind was miles away. Three thousand miles away in Dublin in fact. He was convinced his wife had him committed to a place he described in his manic shouting at the nurses and doctors as "The Gorman", shorthand for Grangegorman mental hospital, an institution he lived in fear of ever spending time in. As soon as he was strong enough to walk, he made his first escape bid while wearing just a pair of hospital pyjamas.

That was the angry sight which greeted Beatrice, Rae Jeffs and George Kleinsinger when they came walking along the corridor to check on him. As he made a go for Beatrice, Jeffs intervened and brought him into a ward to try to convince him he wasn't actually in Dublin. She even had another patient explain to this manic bare-footed figure spewing all sorts of bile that this was a regular hospital in New York where the poor bystander was being treated for a duodenal ulcer. A logical approach to take except Behan wasn't easily convinced.

There was another bid for freedom later that morning. This time, he was only wearing the top half of his pyjamas. Quite the sight as he made a run for it, telling anybody who'd listen he was leaving because they wouldn't give him a drink. Kleinsinger tried his best to persuade the half-naked Behan to return to bed and to find his pants and Beatrice reassured him again and again this was most certainly not Grangegorman. All to no avail. Behan reached the elevator still claiming the hospital was not a hospital but "a puzzle factory". Eventually, Dr. Tasler brought him up in the elevator to one of the higher floors and stood him by a window that offered a spectacular view of the Manhattan skyline.

If that finally convinced him he wasn't in a mental asylum in Ireland, he was still bent on leaving the place. Tasler reasoned with him and they did a deal. He'd stay if the good doctor would bring him a bottle of beer. Hardly recommended medical practice, Tasler thought it was worth bending the rules to keep him where they could treat him. In any case, the contract was soon broken. Behan decided he needed to get out, beer or not, and fast. Now totally frustrated at this man whose life he'd saved the previous day, Tasler gave up and sent somebody to bring the soon-to-be ex-patient the clothes he came in.

"He just got dressed and left, we hadn't even finished the tests," said a hospital spokesman.

Even his departure was freighted with drama. On the way down in the elevator, Behan had a panic attack when he saw a patient on a stretcher. Frantic, he demanded to be let off at the next floor which just happened to be where the cafeteria was located. He approached the counter and asked for a beer. Trying to keep the peace, Kleinsinger whispered to the canteen lady to give him anything that was available. Before she could pour him an apple juice, he was on the move again. He had spotted another woman decanting vinegar from a pitcher into a jar. What happened next would become part of folklore.

He grabbed the pitcher and slurped down the vinegar in almost one go. The poor woman looked shocked. Kleinsinger was horrified. Behan was typically stoic. "It's kind of bitter, George," he said. The type of incident that might be regarded as an urban legend except there were multiple witnesses and he had previous in this regard – John Ryan used to tell a story of him quaffing a bottle of aftershave on a flight one time. At any rate, his hasty departure from the hospital was news.

Newspapers delighted in misreporting that Behan had fled the hospital without the knowledge of the authorities. In one version of the tale, he had called O Henry's restaurant in Greenwich Village and ordered a meal to be sent over. When the delivery boy reached the ward, carrying two sirloins, two baked potatoes and a large salad, Behan's bed was empty and the alarm was raised. The type of story that could easily have happened. That it never did didn't stop it becoming part of the myth.

"Of course, the people at the hospital weren't too keen on his leaving," said Beatrice when a reporter called for an update, "but they couldn't persuade him to stay."

They caught a cab back to the Chelsea where Behan sat in the lobby for a while, not yet fully compos mentis. Indeed, he continued to rant and rave, holding full-scale conversations with himself and imaginary companions, a sight and sound that made his trio of caretakers, now joined by Arthurs, even more worried that he was no longer under medical supervision. Eventually, he was brought up to his room and put to bed at which point his miraculous powers of recovery went to work. He awoke the next morning talking perfect sense. The danger having passed, he had, of course, only one thing on his mind.

Beatrice begged him, yet again, not to hit the bottle. Yet again, he ignored her entreaties and set off for the Oasis, a bar on 23rd Street where the beer cost 15 cents and the owner Willie Garfinkel was the type of old school New York barkeep that Behan loved dealing with. He had company for his day's drinking with Arthurs, George Kleinsinger and Agnes Boulton, wife of the late playwright, Eugene O'Neill, tagging along. Warren Berry, a journalist with the Herald Tribune, popped in as well to conduct an interview. Barely 24 hours after being close to death in intensive care, his life had returned to the old routine, drinking and when there was drinking, there was, inevitably, misbehaviour.

At one point during the day, Behan got into a discussion with Boulton about why her husband had been christened Eugene Gladstone O'Neill. He reckoned it had to have been O'Neill's father James wanting to honour the British Prime Minister William Ewart Gladstone who had introduced reforms that improved the lot of the Irish in the 19th century. However, Behan did not reckon Gladstone worthy of this sort of acknowledgment so he proceeded to lecture Boulton about Anglo-Irish history, growing so agitated as he did that he grabbed her hand and began bending back her fingers to hammer home the point.

If it took the intervention of Arthurs to stop him from going further with the physical assault, the truth is that by now everybody was tired of the Behan show, the propensity for violent rage, the capacity for drunken raimeis, and the ability to create mayhem at a moment's notice. Even Norman Mailer, a man capable of all three of those at any given time himself, admitted that by this point, he and others who'd once enjoyed Behan's company didn't want to be around him anymore.

"He had a need near the end to speak to someone," said Mailer. "He wanted to reach you as if he knew he was going to die. He almost brought out stinginess in you – you didn't want to involve yourself. I have a theory that when a person is dying and he can have a conversation with you, he won't die. Behan knew he had death inside him – he knew that he was ill. But his pride was almost unbearable."

If a lot of those who were happy to indulge his failings when his star was on the rise started to disappear from view, others stepped up. Like many people in the grip of alcoholism, he inclined to let his appearance go and, at one point, stopped shaving. Beatrice implored him to let her get rid of the stubble but he refused. Eventually, Stanley Bard took him into his office, ordered him to take of his shirt and jacket and went at him with shaving foam and a razor. Not a service provided by every hotel but this was the Chelsea, normal rules didn't apply.

Father Peter Jacobs was another not to turn his back on his struggling friend. Over the course of his time in New York, Behan had got to know Jacobs, a Catholic priest with a reputation for an unorthodox approach to his job. Jacobs believed in a pro-active and activist church and spent much of his time working with prisoners, the homeless and the terminally ill. He prided himself on taking confession wherever somebody of faith was willing to speak to him, even if it was at the counter of a bar.

With that kind of resume, it's not surprising he found common ground with Behan. As others flinched at the sight of Behan and recoiled at the thought of his company, Jacobs would walk the streets with him. Sometimes, they would end up sitting on a pier on the North River near 13th Street. Was he hearing his confession during those discussions or just providing a willing ear to a struggling friend? Given the way Jacobs operated, it was most probably a bit of both. Yet, these cameos illustrate how much Behan was struggling with the direction in which his life had gone.

Nobody knew this better than Beatrice. After the debacle of his abortive hospital stay, she was desperate to get him back to Dublin. The only complication with this plan was financial. Tickets to Ireland cost money and the coffers were empty. He had drank away all of the advances, even a reputed $12,000 he received for a history of the Irish struggles against the English, a book he would never write. A visit to the manager of the Manhattan bank where they had an account revealed that the Behans didn't have the price of their passage. This was an enormous come down for a man whose closest friends recalled the ease with which, at the height of his fame, he'd take 500 pounds from the bank before flying to New York.

It was in anticipation of a day just like this that, in happier times, Beatrice had salted away a royalty cheque from "The Hostage" in the deepest recesses of her handbag. The emergency she always feared was at hand. Once cashed, it would be just enough to cover the fares of $240 each. Taking no chances, she proceeded from the bank to the Cunard offices on Park Avenue to book two cabins, one for her and Brendan, the other for Jeffs, on the next sailing of the Queen Elizabeth on July 3rd.

The clock was now ticking on his time in New York. Yet, amazingly, he responded to the imminent departure by getting down to work in tandem with Jeffs over the next few days. Remaining more sober than at any point during the rest of this stay, he sat for two or three sessions of taping per day, seemingly determined to finish the recording that would become "Confessions of an Irish Rebel". If the spirit was willing though, the flesh was weak as even his amanuensis found the material and the delivery dull. There was also the matter of his sinking morale. The nearer the departure date came, the worse his mood got. But his wife was not for turning.

"I was worried about my pregnancy," wrote Beatrice. "I didn't want to stay on in New York until the baby was born. Brendan had tried to persuade me to sell our house in Dublin, which was in my name, and settle in America, but I was just as determined to return to Dublin and equally determined that he should return with me."

In hindsight, some would construe this as a selfish act on her part.

"If he had stayed in America with a new partner, I feel sure he would have recharged his batteries," wrote his brother Brian. "I don't want to sound like I'm blaming Beatrice but if he could have been allowed to end his days in America – where the mantra of 'doing your own thing' always held sway – he could have turned out plays like Niagara Falls. Even if the well of inspiration ran dry, he could have become a 'talking head' on television (the medium after all that made him famous) or turned his hand to writing film scripts."

That opinion ignores the fact that on his last two trips to America, and especially his final visit, he was almost completely incapable of independent work because of his alcoholism, his diabetes and the attendant health problems caused by both diseases. Any literary output from this point onwards came not from pounding the typewriter but from the diligence of Jeffs recording and editing his every utterance to try to fulfill outstanding book contracts. Would a blossoming relationship with Danby-Smith have put him on the dry, living in the city of his dreams? That's quite the stretch.

Still, his heart was undoubtedly heavy on July 3rd when he joined Sean Callery for a farewell drink in Foran's on 23rd Street. Behan sipped a gin as his friend tried not to let on how appalled he was by his physical deterioration. He was in such a state – his shirt was, like himself, in tatters – that Callery surmised he was "a man on the way to the loving arms of Jesus and he wooed death passionately". Other goodbyes were made on less amicable terms. Behan's relationship with Arthurs had degenerated over the course of this visit, so much so that by this time, he was essentially persona non grata. Yet, in the Chelsea that day, he sought Brendan out and found him at the barber shop.

"I held out my hand," wrote Arthurs. "Brendan's eyes remained shut and as tight as a fish's arsehole. His hand remained under the barber's sheet. Finally, one eye opened, a hand begrudgingly crept out, and took hold of mine as though it were an ancient mackerel. 'Goodbye B,' I said. 'Maybe when you get back I will let you read the play that I'm working on but I won't promise. By then you'll almost be a father.' He flinched and tried to pull his hand away. I tightened my grip. 'If it's a boy-child perhaps you'll name him after me, wha'?'... I let go of his hand, turned, opened the door and departed... In my heart of hearts I felt thoroughly sure that I would never see Brendan Behan again."

Behan's sulky and surly demeanour disappeared from view when it came time to step out in public over at the docks that afternoon. At the immigration counter, he was waved through with a smile but Jeffs was stopped and asked what had been the purpose of her visit to New York. "Writing under the name Brendan Behan," he shouted across before she could even answer. The whole room laughed but when the giddiness subsided, he grasped Jeffs' arm as they walked through and whispered, "Few know the truth of that statement!" Beneath the bravado, the insecurity remained. Not that anybody but Jeffs would have known.

"Brendan was a different man by four that afternoon," wrote Callery who had come along to witness the leave-taking. "He held court for the press and the Cunard Line public relations people in a restrained, one might almost say, suave manner. The Daily News photographers succeeded in extracting a conventional bon voyage pose from him, with a broad smile and one arm around his general factotum, Rae Jeffs. A passing priest accepted a drink but good-naturedly declined to bless a tray of cocktails. Brendan allowed that he would do it himself but he was a little shaky on the Latin. His hair was cut and bombed and a presentable suit had replaced the morning's outrageous costume. There was even something like a cultivated cared-for sheen about his complexion. Only the astonishing void where his teeth should have been reminded one that he had not taken the shilling nor slid down the chute onto the Madison Avenue dung-heap."

One more time then, he turned it on for the New York press. Befitting a man heading out of town, he was in the mood to bury the city, not to praise it.

"I think the housing for the working classes is lousy," he said. "Dublin puts you to shame...The buses are filthy in comparison to our buses and the subway is a death-trap... Your newspapers go on forever about nothing."

Beatrice was under no illusions. She realised her husband's dissing of New York was merely him putting on a front, perhaps trying to convince himself it wasn't such a great place after all. She knew the truth of his feelings toward the city was very different.

"It hurt me to realise how heartbroken he was leaving the city of his dreams," wrote Beatrice. "He stayed sober during those last few days so that he would see New York as clearly as on our first visit. But I had turned my face against the city in which he had betrayed me. I had forgiven him but my forgiveness rested on the hope that we could begin our life anew in Dublin."

When the Queen Elizabeth started to move out of the harbour, Beatrice saw her husband staring back at the skyline growing smaller. There was longing and a lingering sadness in his eyes as the city faded from view and he confessed that he knew he'd never see New York again. The heartache of the departure manifested itself in predictable fashion. In the Caribbean Lounge of the Cabin Class section of the ship, he started drinking and mayhem ensued.

The first formal complaint was lodged by a Military Policeman whose new wife had the start of her honeymoon marred by Behan pinching her on the backside. Jeffs, wearing formal evening dress, was about to start eating her first meal of the journey when the stewards came looking for her to help quiet the beast who had moved onto another Cabin Class restaurant where his fellow diners were feeling the full force of his foul tongue.

"I found little comfort from the startled expressions on the faces of the diners as I walked towards the Behan table," wrote Jeffs. "Beatrice, apparently unconcerned, was eating bananas and cream, and while she was delighted to see me she was taking no farther part in the affairs of Brendan. Calling upon the head waiter to help me, we lifted Brendan onto his feet and, supporting him from either side, we half carried him out the door while he flourished the unforgivable word as many times as he could. Once outside, we were beckoned into a nearby cabin to be confronted by the stern face of a senior officer."

The attempt to dress down the drunk wasn't helped by the officer mistakenly addressing him as Brendan Bracken (an Irish-born minister in Winston Churchill's wartime cabinet!). That small matter cleared up, he lambasted Behan and threatened to lock him up for the duration of the rest of the trip. Jeffs tried to point out the futility of the lecture seeing as Behan was almost unconscious by that point, One more time, she came to his rescue, reasoning with the officer, guaranteeing that there would be no further incidents if the officer could, for his part, guarantee the bars would be closed to him until Southampton.

The now comatose Behan was, with great difficulty, carried back to his cabin and sedated by the ship's doctor. What happened next was, in typical Behan fashion, totally unexpected. Once sober and rested, he behaved impeccably for the rest of the voyage, his mood obviously affected for the better by the lack of drink. Indeed, when England hovered into view, many of those on board, crew and passengers, were openly lamenting the fact that their days in the company of the entertaining and genial Behan were over.

There was a curious post-script to the departure. Just over four weeks after the Behans sailed for Southampton, the Pittsburgh Press published an article entitled "To Brendan's Baby". It was an open letter to her unborn child written by Beatrice.

"One day you may read this and understand why your coming is causing a bit of excitement in the world. You and I are going to learn a lot together. You've come late in my life but I'm pleased for all that. There was no reason why I should not have you and I'm glad I waited instead of adopting one. Later I would like you to have brothers and sisters. But there will be problems my child. When you are grown, people will love to say to you, 'I know your father.' Their comments will not always be kind.

When you answer them, remember this, Brendan is a good man, not a phony, no cant, not a trace of snobbery, Irish or otherwise. A man who has been jailed for his principles. A man whose writings are justly world-renowned.

They'll tell you he's a drinker. True enough. But never let them tell you he needs liquor. His good humour prevails with or without it. You'll learn a lot about drinking in your young life, yet Brendan and I do not want you touch a drop until you're 21. You want to concentrate on the dancing and courting, instead of sitting around in bars. Keep to the soft drinks. And after 21? Maybe a drop now and then.

Let me tell you more about Brendan. He's tickled pink at the idea of having you. He's always been very fond of children, is great at romping with them. Children recognise him as a kindred spirit, for Brendan can be as annoying, bold, spoiled, innocent and unafraid as any toddler. Sometimes, he will shout at me, 'Can't you stop the child making so much noise?'

You won't change him but his sheer zest for talk, and language, and song, and his ideas of justice will surely influence you. I love him and he's the most entertaining man I have met. I don't know what I'm going to call you but if you are a boy, it certainly will not be Brendan. There's not room in the world for two.

People often used to say to your father and me, 'Haven't you any children?' Brendan would reply, 'Only me!'

You, Brendan and I are going to have a fine family spirit. They've always been close-knit the Behans, even when your father was across the water in jail, or roistering around the town."

Blanaid Behan was born in Dublin on November 24th, 1963. Her father Brendan died in Dublin on March 20th, 1964. The official causes of death were listed as a hepatic coma and fatty degeneration of the liver, but one American newspaper summed it up more succinctly with the headline, "Bout with bottle ends career".

The day Behan died, his friend and fellow writer Bryan MacMahon was in Iowa City, nearly 5000 miles from Dublin. He learned of Behan's passing when he stepped onto his front porch to pick up his newspaper the next morning. It was headline news. That night, MacMahon was wandering a downtown still caked with snow when he came upon a bookstore. In the window, half of the books had been cleared away and in their place, somebody had put sheets of black paper, in the centre of which stood a half-drunk glass of beer, an empty bottle, an ash-tray, a copy of "The Quare Fellow", and a photograph of Behan.

"I stayed looking at the display for a while," wrote MacMahon. "It was a fair tribute in the American manner. About me the street was empty and the smell of pizza and coffee was strong in the frosted air. Then I smiled; the beer bottle was British Bass, a drink that, due to an alleged anti-Irish statement by one of the directors, the IRA had tried to outlaw in Ireland. 'Will I change it?' the girl in the bookstore asked when I told her of it. 'No,' I said. 'Brendan would have liked the irony of the tribute.' So we let it stand."

Acknowledgements

In a thrift store on the north shore of Long Island some years back, I bought a biography of Brendan Behan by Michael O'Sullivan, for no other reason than it was the only Irish book in the place. I put it on a shelf and promised myself I'd get around to reading it some day. Eighteen months ago, I belatedly started into what is a remarkable study of an extraordinary life. By the time I'd finished O'Sullivan's book, I wanted to know more, lots more, about Behan's time in America.

The result of that curiosity is in your hands today thanks to PJ Cunningham at Ballpoint Press, an editor whose enthusiasm, encouragement and support for this project was infectious. Equally, I'm grateful to Joe Coyle for bringing his exceptional design skills to bear and turning the manuscript into such a beautiful book.

As per cliché, there are too many other people to thank but it would be remiss of me not to express my gratitude to Cosimo Bassi, Letty Cottin Pogrebin, Colm O'Callaghan, Enda McEvoy, Paul Howard, Denis Walsh, Tommy Conlon, PJ Browne, Dave Clarke and Michael Foley for assisting in different ways along the road. Professor Clare Frost of Stony Brook University was kind enough to take time off from her well-deserved retirement to proofread the first draft. She saved me from many errors and any mistakes that remain are, of course, my own.

Almost twenty-five years have passed since I walked into UCC and started to hang around with Gavin O'Connor, Emmet Barry, Mark Penney, Ken Cotter, Mark O'Loughlin and Fergus Roche. The callow-faced teenagers are (almost!) middle-aged men now but true friendship has endured in the most wonderful way, across the decades and across the oceans. For supporting this project, like they have all the others, I thank them.

Nineteen years have passed since I walked into the kitchen of the Frost family home on Long Island and announced myself as their daughter Cathy's Irish fella. For everything they have done for us both since then, and for the support they give me every day, I thank George and Clare Frost.

For supplying all that over a longer period, I thank my brother Tom, sister Denise, and niece Kadie. My father Denis died some years ago but he is the reason I started to read books and to write them. He put the Hardy Boys in my hands, he bought me SHOOT! magazine, and he offered me the example of a man who loved to get lost in a good book. I owe him and my incredible mother Theresa a debt I can never repay.

Finally, I would like to thank my wife Cathy. For 14 years she has been battling physical illnesses that would have broken a lesser person. Her courage in the face of so much adversity is a constant inspiration and something that puts moaning about book deadlines into proper context on a daily basis. I would also like to especially thank her for giving me Abe, Charlie and Finn, the three darling boys who make every day in our household impossibly loud, hugely entertaining and always action-packed. They are the lights of my life.

East Setauket, New York
February, 2014

Select Bibliography

Books

Arthurs, Peter, With Brendan Behan, New York: St. Martin's Press, 1981

Aspler, Tony, Travels with my Corkscrew, Toronto: McGraw Hill, 1997

Behan, Beatrice, My Life with Brendan, Los Angeles, Nash Publishing, 1974

Behan, Brendan, Brendan Behan's New York, New York, Geis, 1964

Behan, Brendan, The Letters of Brendan Behan, Montreal: McGill-Queen's University Press, 1992

Behan, Brendan, The Complete Plays, London, Methuen, 1978

Behan, Brian and Dillon-Malone, A, The Brothers Behan, Dublin: Ashfield Press, 1998

Boyle, Ted Eugene, Brendan Behan, New York: Twayne Publishers, 1969

Cheever, John and Cheever, Benjamin, The Letters of John Cheever, New York: Simon and Schuster, 1988

Cheever, Susan, Note Found in a Bottle, New York: Simon and Schuster, 1999

Friendly, Fred W, Due to Circumstances Beyond our Control, New York: Random House, 1967

Grey, Frank, The Crazy Life of Brendan Behan. Milton Keynes: Authorhouse, 2010

Hamilton, Ed, Legends of the Chelsea Hotel, Cambridge: Da Capo, 2007

Hemingway, Valerie, Running with the Hemingways, New York: Ballantine Books, 2004

Jeffs, Rae, Brendan Behan – Man and Showman, London: Hutchison, 1966

Kearney, Colbert, The Writings of Brendan Behan, New York: St. Martin's Press, 1977

Kelley, Robin, Thelonious Monk – The life and times of an American original, New York: Simon and Schuster, 2009

Levin, Bernard, The way we live now, London: Cape, 1984

Littlewood, Joan, Joan's Book, London: Methuen, 1994

Lennon, J Michael, Norman Mailer – A Double Life, New York: Simon and Schuster, 2013

Lyons, Jeffrey, Stories my father told me, New York: Abbeville Press, 2011

Marx, Groucho, The Groucho Letters, New York: Simon and Schuster, 1967

McCann, Sean, The Wit of Brendan Behan, London: Frewin, 1968

McCann, Sean, The World of Brendan Behan, New York: Twayne Publishers, 1966

McCourt, Malachy, A Monk Swimming, New York: Hyperion, 1998

Meredith, Burgess, So Far, So Good, New York: Little Brown, 1994

Mikhail, E.H, Brendan Behan: interviews and recollections Vol 1, London: Macmillan, 1982

Mikhail, E.H, Brendan Behan: interviews and recollections Vol 2, London: Macmillan, 1982

Mikhail, E.H, The Letters of Brendan Behan, London: Macmillan, 1992

Miller, Arthur, Timebends, A Life, New York: Grove Press, 1997

O'Connor, Ulick, Brendan Behan, London: Hamilton, 1970

O'Sullivan, Michael, Brendan Behan – A Life, Dublin: Blackwater Press, 1999

Paar, Jack, My Saber is Bent, New York, Trident Press, 1961

Parish, James Robert, The Seriously Funny Life of Mel Brooks, Hoboken: Wiley, 2007

Pogrebin, Letty Cottin, How to Make it in a Man's World, New York: Doubleday, 1970

Rotolo, Suze, A Freewheelin' Time: A memoir of Greenwich Village in the sixties, New York: Broadway Books, 2008

Spinetti, Victor, Up Front, London, Robson Books, 2006

Tippins, Sherill, Inside the Dream Palace: The Life and Times of New York's Legendary Chelsea Hotel, Boston, Houghton Mifflin, 2013

Newspapers and Magazines

Catskill Mountain News, Commonweal, Daytona Beach Morning Journal, Esquire, Grand Street, Lawrence Journal-World, LIFE, Los Angeles Times, Milwaukee Sentinel, Montreal Gazette, New York Times, The New Yorker, New York, New York Herald Tribune, Newsweek, New York Post, New York Daily News, Ottawa Citizen, Pittsburgh Press, Reading Eagle, St. Petersburg Times, Sumter Daily Item, Time. Toronto Star, Vassar Miscellany News

Academic Paper

Clare, David, The Disputed Authorship of Brendan Behan's The Hostage, EGS Seminar Series, UCD, February, 2012

Discography

Brendan Behan: Irish Folk Songs and Ballads, Spoken Arts SA 760

Brendan Behan: On Joyce, Folkway Records

Documentary

A Hungry Feeling: The life and death of Brendan Behan, Allan Miller, 1988

Index

About The Author

Dave Hannigan is a columnist with the Evening Echo (Cork) and the Irish Echo (New York), and an adjunct professor at Suffolk County Community College and Stony Brook University. Born in Cork, he now lives in East Setauket, Long Island with his wife Cathy, and sons, Abe, Charlie and Finn. This is his eighth book.